A READER'S MANIFESTO

A READER'S MANIFESTO

An Attack on the Growing Pretentiousness
in American Literary Prose

by B.R. Myers

 Melville House

Hoboken, New Jersey
2002

Melville House Publishing
P.O. Box 3278
Hoboken, NJ 07030

Design: Deb Wood

ISBN 0-9718659-0-6

SECOND PRINTING, OCTOBER 2002

LIBRARY OF CONGRESS CATALOGING-IN-PUBLICATION DATA

MYERS, B. R., 1963-
A READER'S MANIFESTO : AN ATTACK ON THE GROWING PRETENTIOUSNESS
IN AMERICAN LITERARY PROSE / B. R. MYERS.— 1ST ED.
P. CM.
INCLUDES BIBLIOGRAPHICAL REFERENCES.
ISBN 0-9718659-0-6
1. AMERICAN PROSE LITERATURE—HISTORY AND CRITICISM—THEORY, ETC.
I.
TITLE.
PS362 .M94 2002
818'.08—DC21

2002010795

TABLE OF CONTENTS

FOR MYUNGHEE

Those who write preciously are like people who get dolled up to avoid being confused and confounded with the mob, a danger run by no gentleman even in the worst clothes. As a certain sartorial pomp...betrays the plebeian, so does a precious style betray the commonplace mind.

Schopenhauer

In late 1999 I wrote a short book called *Gorgons in the Pool*. Quoting lengthy passages from prize-winning novels, I argued that some of the most acclaimed contemporary prose is the product of mediocre writers availing themselves of trendy stylistic gimmicks. The greater point was that we readers should trust our own taste and perception instead of deferring to received opinion. A banal thing to say? I only wish it was. For the past few decades our cultural establishment has propagated a very different message. The poet Philip Larkin once gave it this sardonic summing-up:

> The terms and the arguments vary with the circumstances, but basically the message is: Don't trust your eyes, or ears, or understanding. They'll tell you this is ridiculous, or ugly, or meaningless. Don't believe them. You've got to work at this: after all, you don't expect to understand anything as important as art straight off, do you? I mean, this is pretty complex stuff: if you want to know how complex, I'm giving a course of ninety-six lectures at the local college, starting next week. [1]

And indeed, one of the main complaints later raised against me by *The New York Times* was that I bring only my "own sensibility to bear" instead of interpreting literature in the context of "economics, history and sociology."[2] The ninety-six lectures, in other words. But I'm getting ahead of myself.

If anything has less chance of being accepted for publication than an amateur book review, it is an amateur literary polemic. From the start, therefore, I assumed there was no point submitting *Gorgons in the Pool* to publishers. In March 2000 I printed a hundred copies myself and posted the title on Amazon.com, the online bookseller. Then I sent twenty review copies to newspapers and magazines around the English-speaking world, in the hope that someone at a safe enough remove from New York City would acknowledge the book with a review. Then I sat back and waited. Nothing happened. I went online and ordered three copies of *Gorgons* for myself; they were the only ones ever sold. By the end of spring I had pushed the remainder of the first edition under my couch and was trying hard to think about something else. I had almost succeeded when in July 2000 Bill Whitworth, editor emeritus of *The Atlantic Monthly*, wrote to tell me that he had enjoyed *Gorgons* and had passed it on to his colleagues. A few days later Mike Kelly, the magazine's new editor, called to ask if I would let him run an abridged form of the book in an upcoming issue. I said yes. Needless to say, it would have been much more gratifying to see *Gorgons* succeed on its own, but what choice did I have, with no money for advertising? It wasn't as if anyone was ever going to review the thing. (A few days later *The Times Literary Supplement* contacted me to inquire after *Gorgons*' sales price; they were going to run a review the following Sunday. I had to beg them not to, having promised *The Atlantic Monthly* that I would take the book off the market. There's an obvious lesson here, but it's still a little hard for me to talk about.)

The next few weeks were spent cutting *Gorgons* in half. Out went the examples of good prose from writers like Balzac. This had the unfortunate result of making the tone almost unrelentingly negative, so that at half the length of the book it feels like twice as long a read. But improvements were made too. *The Atlantic*'s copy-editors found many mistakes in the manuscript, including misquotes of the literary texts. I was starting to think it was just as well that *Gorgons* was no longer on sale when I received the first galleys in August 2000, and saw that crucial phrases and passages had been deleted, apparently in order to tone the whole thing down. Even the sex scene from *Snow Falling on Cedars* was gone. When I called to complain, I was told that there had just been another editorial meeting, the upshot of which was that my essay needed to be made even more "serious and developed." I said no. It had been written as a light-hearted polemic, and to trick it out as literary scholarship would only make it more vulnerable to criticism.

The folks at *The Atlantic* said they'd get back to me. They didn't, nor did they answer my e-mails. Months passed. In January 2001 I wrote to suggest that we all walk away from the contract. This got the dialogue going again, and we started to compromise: I would refrain from saying that Michiko Kakutani had no right to review books if they would give me back my sex scene, and so on. Oddly enough, the final product was billed on the cover flap of the July/August 2001 issue as "A Reader's Manifesto about the GODAWFULNESS of today's literary writing," which was a little strong even for me.

This book, then, is an attempt to restore *Gorgons in the Pool* to its original tone and length while retaining the improvements, starting with the title, of the magazine version. As in *Gorgons* I briefly contrast the writing of DeLillo, Proulx, etc with that of non-contemporary writers like Honoré de Balzac and Thomas Wolfe. I have no intention of suggesting that any of the latter were unequalled masters of prose — only that they wrote far better than today's prize-winners on comparable themes or in comparable styles. All the same, I have no doubt that the same people who criticized the magazine version for not offering enough examples of good prose will be the first to complain that I am now comparing apples to oranges, since no two writers are alike. But Keith Haring and Pablo Picasso had less in common than DeLillo and Balzac, and this doesn't prevent anyone from calling Picasso the better artist of the two.

This book also contains an entirely new section in which I respond to the attempts at rebutting the magazine version that were published last year.

I would like to use this space to acknowledge a debt of inspiration to Karlheinz Deschner's *Kitsch, Konvention und Kunst: Eine literarische Streitschrift* (Munich, 1957). I would also like to thank Keith Myers for editing the original *Gorgons*; Bill Whitworth, Sue Parilla, Ben Schwarz, Mike Kelly and everyone else at *The Atlantic Monthly* who worked on the magazine essay; and Haechin Moon for her suggestions regarding the new material in this book. I have already replied to most of my fellow readers who wrote me about the magazine essay, as well as to the writers who were kind enough to send me copies of their own work, but if you never got anything back from me, please accept my sincere thanks now. I am especially grateful to Dennis Loy Johnson and Melville House for taking on this book, and for understanding the concept so well. Most of all, I would like to thank my agent and friend Theresa Park.

B. R. Myers

A READER'S MANIFESTO

INTRODUCTION

Nothing gives me the feeling of having been born several decades too late quite like the modern "literary" best seller. Give me a time-tested masterpiece or what critics patronizingly call a fun read, *Sister Carrie* or just plain *Carrie*. Give me anything, in fact, as long as it isn't the latest must-read novel, complete with a prize jury's seal of approval on the front and a clutch of precious raves on the back. In the bookstore I'll sometimes sample what all the fuss is about, but one glance at the affected prose — "furious dabs of tulips stuttering,"[3] say, or "in the dark before the day yet was"[4] — and I'm hightailing it to the friendly black spines of the Penguin Classics.

I realize that such a declaration must sound perversely ungrateful to the cultural establishment. For years now editors, critics and prize jurors, not to mention novelists themselves, have been telling the rest of us how lucky we are to be alive and reading in these exciting times. The absence of a dominant school of criticism, we are told, has resulted in an unlimited variety of styles, a smorgasbord with something for every palate. As novelist and critic David Lodge has remarked, "everything is in and nothing is out."[5] But in fact, criticism is far more prescriptive today than it was in the first half of the twentieth century. Back then Christopher Isherwood and Somerset Maugham were both ranked among the finest novelists in the English language and considered no less literary in their own way than Virginia Woolf and James Joyce. Today, any accessible story written in unaffected prose is deemed to be *genre fiction*; at best an excellent "read" or "page turner," but never literature with a capital L. Everything written in self-conscious, writerly prose, on the other hand, is *literary fiction* — not necessarily *good* literary fiction, mind you, but always worthier of respect and full-page reviews than even the best thriller or romance.

Our "literary" writers aren't expected to evince much in the way of brain power. Musing about consumerism, bandying about words like "ontological," chanting *Red River* hokum as if it were a lost book of the Old Testament: this is what passes for intellectual content today. Nor do writers need a poet's sensibility or sharp eye. It is the departure from natural speech that counts, not what, if anything, is being arrived at. A sufficiently obtrusive idiom can even induce critics to overlook the sin of a strong plot. Conversely, though more rarely, a concise prose style can be pardoned if a novel's pace is slow enough, as was the case with Ha Jin's aptly titled *Waiting*, which won the National Book Award in 1999.

The dualism of literary versus genre has all but routed the old trinity of highbrow, middlebrow and lowbrow, which had always been invoked tongue in cheek anyway. Novelists who would once have been called middlebrow are now assigned on the basis of their verbal affectation to either the "literary" or the "genre" camp. David Guterson is thus granted Serious Writer status on the basis of *Snow Falling on Cedars* (1994), a murder mystery buried under sonorous tautologies, while Stephen

3

King, whose *Bag of Bones* (1998) is a more intellectual but less pretentious novel, is still considered to be just a talented storyteller. Everything is "in," in other words, as long as it keeps the reader at a respectful distance.

This may seem an odd trend in view of the decades-long decline in the quality of English instruction at our schools and colleges. Shouldn't a dumbed-down America be more willing to confer literary status on straightforward prose, instead of encouraging affectation and obscurity? Not necessarily. In Aldous Huxley's *Those Barren Leaves* (1925) a character named Mr. Cardan offers an explanation for this apparent paradox:

> Really simple, primitive people like their poetry to be as...artificial and remote from the language of everyday affairs as possible. We reproach the eighteenth century with its artificiality. But the fact is that *Beowulf* is couched in a diction fifty times more complicated and unnatural than that of [Pope's poem] *Essay on Man*.[6]

Mr. Cardan comes off in the novel as a bit of a windbag, but there is at least anecdotal evidence to back up his observation. We know that European peasants were far from pleased when their clergy stopped mystifying them with Latin. Edward Pococke (1604-1691) was an English preacher and linguist whose sermons, according to the *Oxford Book of Literary Anecdotes*, "were always composed in plain style upon practical subjects, carefully avoiding all show and ostentation of learning."

> But from this very exemplary caution not to amuse his hearers (contrary to the common

method then in vogue) with what they could not understand, some of them took occasion to entertain very contemptible thoughts of his learning...So that one of his Oxford friends, as he traveled through Childrey, inquiring for his diversion of some of the people, Who was their minister, and how they liked him? received this answer: "Our parson is one Mr. Pococke, a plain honest man. But Master," said they, "he is no Latiner."[7]

Of course I'm not calling anyone a peasant, but neither am I prepared to believe that the decline of American literacy has affected everyone but fans of so-called serious fiction. When reviewers tout a repetitive style as "the last word in gnomic control," or a jumble of unsustained metaphor as "lyrical" writing, it is obvious that they too are having difficulty understanding what they read. Would Mr. Cardan be surprised to find them in the thrall of writers who are deliberately obscure, or who chant in strange cadences? I doubt it. Nor would he be surprised to find unaffected English dismissed today as "workmanlike prose," an idiom incompatible with real literature. Stephen King's a plain, honest man, just the author to read on the subway. But Master, he is no Latiner.

Don't get me wrong. I agree with the British critic Cyril Connolly that we need the "Mandarin" artifice of Woolf and Joyce as much as we need the "Vernacular" straightforwardness of Isherwood and Hemingway.[8] The problem with so much of today's literature is the *clumsiness* of its artifice — the conspicuous disparity between what writers are aiming for and what they actually achieve. Theirs is a remarkably crude form of affectation: a prose so repetitive, so elementary in its syntax, and so numbing in its overuse of wordplay that it often demands less concentration than the average "genre" novel. Even today's obscurity is easy, the sort of gibberish that stops all thought dead in its tracks.

This may not be the only thing wrong with contemporary fiction, but to discuss matters of plot or character development is to prevent readers unfamiliar with the works in question from following the discussion as critically as they should. Besides, we can all argue about whether a story is interesting or a character believable, but few literate people would deny that "a clash of sound, discordant," is repetitive, or that "from whence there could be no way back" is absurdly archaic for a story set in the Truman years.

This makes it even more remarkable that our nation's critics should be so reluctant to discuss prose style. Just compare the amateur book reviews on Amazon to the reviews in major newspapers. The amateurs keep the story to themselves, so as not to spoil the fun for others, and tend to make frank recommendations based on how the writer expresses himself: directly or pretentiously, clearly or obscurely, and so on. Most of the average *New York Times* review, on the other hand, is devoted to describing the cast of characters and giving away the plot. Virtually nothing is said about the writer's style, even when, as is often the case, it is held up as the best part of the book under review. This is typical:

> Fundamentally, Mr. Doig is a writer we read less for anything new that he expresses than for his new and stylish expression; though it serves the conventional wisdom, his is a prose as tight as a new thread and as special as handmade candy. (Lee Abbott)[9]

Critics seem to have a hard time discussing prose in a straightforward manner — finding a middle ground, in other words, between stodgy academic jargon and twee comparisons to hand-made candy. At best they will quote one or two sentences from the text, usually the most stilted ones they can find, along with some empty remark like "now *that's* great writing." An increasingly common practice is to print excerpts in their own little boxes, with no commentary at all. The implication is clear enough: "If you don't know why that's great, I won't waste my time trying to explain."

Are critics avoiding the subject of prose, the better to praise novels which they know are badly written? Perhaps. Europeans are often struck by the self-protectiveness of the American literary scene, and even insiders admit that friendship-mongering is rampant.[10] At the very least it seems safe to say that book reviewers, most of whom are novelists in their own right, have a hard time emulating the frankness of film and theater critics. Herbert Gold tells how he began to review a book by acknowledging his friendship with the writer:

> The book-review editor rejected my notice by saying, "we don't admit friendship plays any part in reviewing. If it does, we don't admit it." And it was also clear that he was rejecting *me* for betraying the charade of objectivity.[11]

Once Gold received galleys of a new novel along with a form letter from the publisher.

> He introduced it by saying it was "by the fre-

7

> quent reviewer X," with a clear implication:
> Now your novelist to praise, tomorrow per-
> haps your very own reviewer ... When the pub-
> lisher printed my comment on the book jack-
> et, he deleted my accusation of blackmail. [12] *

Of course it's one thing to say that this goes on, and another to point the finger at a rave review without evidence. When Jay McInerney praises Don DeLillo's "analytic rigor," I have to assume that he means it. [13]

I have kept this book short in the assumption that a brief look at five contemporary novelists will suffice to show at least part of what is wrong with American prose at the turn of the millennium. I have chosen Paul Auster, Don DeLillo, David Guterson, Cormac McCarthy and Annie Proulx not because I bear them any malice, but because each has received overwhelmingly favorable reviews, been honored with at least one literary award, and sold well over five hundred thousand copies. All but DeLillo have recently seen their novels made into movies. Just as importantly, each represents a different faction within the fold of modern prose. McCarthy's fondness for archaism, for example, is shared by numerous writers today, as is Proulx's overuse of metaphor. I should make clear, however, that these five all write either at or slightly above the average level of contemporary prose. While it might be considered fairer (and more entertaining) to deal with a handful of truly awful obscurities, this would do nothing to prove either the existence of a trend or the cultural establishment's role in encouraging it.

Needless to say, my opinions derive from reading entire novels; the excerpts in this book are provided to explain these opinions to readers. To forestall charges of

* All elliptical points in quotations are mine unless stated otherwise.

seeking out isolated howlers, a practice rightly dismissed by Evelyn Waugh as "the badger digging of literary blood sports,"[14] I have drawn as much material as possible from opening chapters, which tend to reflect writers at their best, and from passages already quoted by admiring reviewers and scholars. Nothing is quoted that is not representative of the writer in question. Anyone who doubts me on this is welcome to read all the excerpted books, and all the excerpted journalism for that matter, from start to finish.

One more thing. Back in the old days, when there was still some Holden Caulfield in the national psyche, the greatest sin was held to be pretension. Now it is the unassuming storyteller who is reviled, while mediocrities who puff themselves up to produce gabby "literary" fiction are guaranteed a certain respect, presumably for aiming high. I make no apology for flouting this convention, i.e., for discussing so-called literary novelists in a tone that *The New York Times* likes to reserve for mocking Jackie Collins. It is as easy to aim high as to aim low. Isn't it time we went back to judging writers on whether they hit the mark?

EVOCATIVE PROSE

"Poetry has gone through a bad patch and severe discipline has been necessary to write it; consequently others who start out with only facility, sensibility and a lyrical outlook, rather than undergo the hardships of training, have allowed their poetical feeling to relax in prose."[15] This is truer today than when Cyril Connolly wrote it in 1938, for it has never been more fashionable to exploit the license of poetry while begging a novelist's exemption from precision and polish. The leading exponent of this style is Annie Proulx, who gives us a taste of it in the acknowledgments to her short story anthology *Close Range* (1999):

> Most of all, deepest thanks to my children for putting up with my strangled, work-driven ways.[16]

That's right: strangled, work-driven ways. *Work-driven* is fine of course, except for its note of self-approval, but *strangled ways* makes no sense on any level. The resemblance to "stunted means (of education)," Fowler's example of bad metaphor, is striking. "Education (personifed) may be stunted," he wrote, "but means may not."[17] Nor can ways be strangled, let alone strangled and work-driven at the same time. Perhaps Proulx meant something along the lines of a nightly smackdown with the Muse, but only she knows for sure. Luckily for her, there are many readers out there who expect literary language to be so remote from their own tongue as to be routinely incomprehensible. "Strangled ways," they murmur to themselves in baffled admiration, "now who but a Writer would think of that!"

And it just gets better and better. The first story in *Close Range* is "The Half-Skinned Steer," which John Updike, carrying on the entertaining tradition of good writers with bad taste, considers one of the best American short stories of the twentieth century.[18] It starts with one of the most highly praised sentences of the past ten years:

> In the long unfurling of his life, from tight-wound kid hustler in a wool suit riding the train out of Cheyenne to geriatric limper in this spooled-out year, Mero had kicked down thoughts of the place where he began, a so-called ranch on strange ground at the south hinge of the Big Horns.[19]

A conceit must have been intended here, but "unfurling" or spreading-out, as of a flag or umbrella, clashes disastrously with the images of thread which follow. (Presumably "unraveling" didn't sound literary enough.) A life is "unfurled," a man is "wound tight," a year is "spooled out," and still the barrage of metaphors continues with "kicked down," which might work in less crowded surroundings, though I doubt it, and "hinge," which is cute if you've never seen a hinge or a map of the Big Horns. And this is just the first sentence! Like so much writing today it demands to be read quickly, with just enough attention to note the bold use of words. Slow down, and things fall apart.

With good Mandarin prose the opposite is true.

When Saul Bellow writes in *Augie March* (1953) of "heavy black hair slipping back loose and tuberous from a topknot,"[20] the word *tuberous* seems contrived at first, but you need only visualize the thick, rounded part of a root to realize how perfect it is. Bellow follows this with "drinking coffee, knitting, reading, painting her nails," etcetera, because good writers know that verbal innovation derives its impact from the contrast to straightforward language. Even Joyce's *Finnegans Wake* (1939) has a "normal" stretch in it. But Proulx's wordplay virtually never lets up; it is hard to find three consecutive sentences in which she isn't trying to startle or impress the reader. Often more than one metaphor is devoted to the same image:

> Furious dabs of tulips stuttering in gardens. [21]

> An apron of sound lapped out of each dive. [22]

> The children rushed at Quoyle, gripped him as a falling man clutches the window ledge, as a stream of electric particles arcs a gap and completes a circuit.[23]

> The ice mass leaned as though to admire its reflection in the waves, leaned until the southern tower was at the angle of a pencil in a writing hand, the northern tower reared over it like a lover.[24]

On the second page of *The Shipping News* Proulx introduces the central character as a man with a body like a loaf of bread, a head like a melon, facial features like fingertips, eyes the color of plastic and a chin like a shelf.[25] The reader is left trying to care about a walking Arcimboldo painting.

This isn't all bad, of course; the b[...]
mass admiring its reflection would be e[...]
weren't ruined by the laborious similes that f[...]
every so often Proulx lets a really good image stan[...]

> The dining room, crowded with men, was lit
> by red bulbs that gave them a look of being
> roasted alive in their chairs. [26]

Such hits are so rare, however, that after a while the reader
stops trying to think about what the metaphors mean.
Perhaps this is the very effect Proulx is aiming for; she seems
to want to keep us on the surface of the text at all times, lest
we forget her quirky presence for even a line or two.

But how to keep the focus on style even during the
nuts-and-bolts work of exposition? How to get to the next
metaphor-laden passage as fast as possible without
resorting to straightforwardness, that dreaded idiom of
the genre hack? Proulx's solution is an obtrusively ugly
— and therefore "literary" — telegraphese:

> Made a show of taking Quoyle back as a special
> favor. Temporary.... Fired, car wash atten-
> dant, rehired. Fired, cabdriver, rehired. [27]

> Sliced purple tomato. Changed the talk to
> descriptions of places he had been, Strabane,
> South Amboy, Clark Fork. In Clark Fork had
> played pool with a man with a deviated sep-
> tum. Wearing kangaroo gloves. [28]

By now the reader will have noticed that while
this is wearying writing it is far from complex, especially
not when compared to the Mandarin syntax of the past.

t about the ice
fective if it
llow. And
d alone:

warmth and eloquence, she
quity of the English dairy sys-
state milk was delivered at
about to prove her charges,
into the matter, when all
, beginning with Andrew in the
middle, like a fire leaping from tuft to tuft of
furze, her children laughed; her husband
laughed; she was laughed at, fire encircled, and
forced to veil her crest, dismount her batteries,
and only retaliate by displaying the raillery
and ridicule of the table to Mr. Bankes as an
example of what one suffered if one attacked
the prejudices of the British public.[29]

You have to concentrate on such prose; miss even one
clause and you have to go back and start again. But
today's pseudo-Mandarins are no more able to write such
syntax than their fans are willing to follow it. Sure, Proulx
has plenty of long sentences, but they are usually little
more than lists:

> Partridge black, small, a restless traveler
> across the slope of life, an all-night talker;
> Mercalia, second wife of Partridge and the
> color of a brown feather on dark water, a hot
> intelligence; Quoyle large, white, stumbling
> along, going nowhere. [30]

Black, *small*, *large* and *white* are perfunctory, inexpressive
adjectives. For all its *faux* precision that feather simile is

14

ultimately meaningless; there are too many different shades of brown to evoke whatever color Proulx had in mind (even with "dark water" under it). A more conventional prose style — "Partridge was a small, black man who talked all night," for example — would show up the poverty of observation at once, but by running a dozen dull attributes together Proulx can ensure that each is seen only in the context of a flashy whole. This technique, which calls to mind a bad photographer hurrying through a slide-show, is the key to most of her supposedly lyrical effects. In this scene a woman has just had her arms sliced off by a piece of sheet metal:

> She stood there, amazed, rooted, seeing the grain of the wood of the barn clapboards, paint jawed away by sleet and driven sand, the unconcerned swallows darting and reappearing with insects clasped in their beaks looking like mustaches, the wind-ripped sky, the blank windows of the house, the old glass casting blue swirled reflections at her, the fountains of blood leaping from her stumped arms, even, in the first moment, hearing the wet thuds of her forearms against the barn and the bright sound of the metal striking. (*Accordion Crimes*) [31]

The last thing Proulx wants is for you to start wondering whether someone with blood spurting from severed arms is going to stand "rooted" long enough to see more than one bird disappear, catch an insect, and reappear, or whether the whole scene is not in bad taste of the juvenile variety. Instead you are meant to run your eyes down the page and succumb, under the sheer accumulation of words, to a spurious impression of what *The New York Times*' Walter Kendrick calls "brilliant prose" (and in reference to this very excerpt, besides).[32]

These slide-shows take place on almost every other page, but in the interests of fairness let's look at another one singled out for praise by both *The New York Times* (in this case Richard Eder) and *Time*.[33] This is from "The Mud Below," a short story in *Close Range*:

> Pake knew a hundred dirt road short cuts, steering them through scabland and slope country, in and out of the tiger shits, over the tawny plain still grooved with pilgrim wagon ruts, into early darkness and the first storm laying down black ice, hard orange dawn, the world smoking, snaking dust devils on bare dirt, heat boiling out of the sun until the paint on the truck hood curled, ragged webs of dry rain that never hit the ground, through small-town traffic and stock on the road, band of horses in the morning fog, two redheaded cowboys moving a house that filled the roadway and Pake busting around and into the ditch to get past, leaving junkyards and Mexican cafés behind, turning into midnight motel entrances with RING OFFICE BELL signs or steering onto the black prairie for a stunned hour of sleep. [34]

There are good bits in there, to be sure, like the "webs of dry rain that never hit the ground," but not enough to make up for the incongruity of style. This is a long, mid-summer truck trip across the plains, a trip which the characters themselves apparently find dull and uneventful, and it receives the same breathless treatment as the twenty seconds of spurting blood in *Accordion Crimes*. Why? Because Proulx is too egocentric to put herself in her characters' shoes, even if she does sprinkle her text with enough regional slang, foreign words and other frippery to make *The New York Times* think that she "grapples herself to her people."[35] "Tiger shits," for example, sounds like something a Pake might say, and it has the added advantage of being incomprehensible. The rest of that description has Yankee Tourist written all over it, and I don't mean just those "pilgrim wagon ruts." No one native to the region would think of house-movers as cowboys, nor would the occupants of that truck care about the hair color of two men passed at high speed in a ditch. So why should we care either? There's plenty of irrelevant detail in Dickens too, and in Sterne and Gogol too, but at least it is imaginative and interesting. Not like this:

> [Chris] wore a pair of dark glasses and began to run with a bunch of *cholos*, especially with a rough called "*Venas*," a black mole on his left nostril, someone who poured money into his white Buick with the crushed velvet upholstery, whose father, Paco Robelo, the whole Robelo family, were rumored to be connected with *narcotraficantes*.
>
> In a year or two Chris had his own car, a secondhand Chevrolet repainted silver, with painted flames....[36]

As usual, the Proulxian lens is given a light dusting of authentic-looking vocabulary — in this case, Spanish words drawn unthinkingly from the dictionary. ("*Narcotraficantes*" sounds as incongruous in this context as the word "drug-traffickers" would sound in a trailer

17

park.) We hear no more of Venas until several years and pages later, when an offhand sentence informs us that he was found clubbed to death. We're evidently not meant to wonder who did it or why, or how the death affects Chris. So why did we need to know the exact location of Venas' mole? His father's first name? If the lapping aprons are fake Dylan Thomas, an effort to mystify readers into thinking they are reading poetry, then this is fake Dos Passos, cheap detail flung in for the illusion of panoramic sweep.

It's a shame really, because by chattering on about everything from the pattern on a Band-Aid to the smell of "Sierra Free dish detergent scented with calendula and horsemint,"[37] Proulx drowns out occasional details that are well-observed, such as the information, which is somehow both funny and sad at the same time, that a man's cheap wet socks have dyed his toenails blue. Someone needs to tell her that half of good writing is knowing what to leave out.

But such an acclaimed writer can hardly be blamed for thinking, "If it ain't broke, why fix it?" Her novel *Postcards* (1992) received the PEN/Faulkner Award in 1993; *The Shipping News* won both the National Book Award (1993) and the Pulitzer Prize (1994). At least some of this success seems to derive from the appeal of her regional settings and characters. Carolyn See compares the Wyoming of *Close Range* to a "gorgeous, abusive spouse. You don't ever want to leave him unless you have to, but" — postfeminist chuckle — "you just might have to."[38] Plenty of urban intellectuals, it seems, would rather smile on an affectionately stylized cowboy underclass than admit that rednecks are the same dreary bullies west of the Mississippi as east of it. Even the hokiest aphorisms are held up for admiration:

> "Well," says an acquaintance [in *Close Range*], "you rodeo, you're a rooster on Tuesday, a feather-duster on Wednesday." On that line Proulx gains the crossroads of great writing, the intersection of the specific and the universal, of the fate offered by her upland Wyoming and by the human condition at large. (Richard Eder, *The New York Times*.)[39]

I know what you're thinking. I thought so too for a second. Believe me, the man is serious.

But it is undeniably the sheer bizarreness of Proulx's writing that wins her the most points, thereby confirming Evelyn Waugh's assertion that "professional reviewers read so many bad books in the course of duty that they get an unhealthy craving for arresting phrases."[40] No one really cares what the words mean; "apron of sound" is startling, therefore it is good — or rather, "evocative" and "compelling," conveniently vague attributes that have become *the* literary catchwords of our time. Nor does anyone mind the lack of polish. *Time*'s John Skow wrote the following in approval of *Close Range*:

> Annie Proulx twirls words like a black-hat badman twirling Colts, fires them off for the sheer hell of it, blam, blam, no thought of missing, empty beer cans jump in the dust, misses one, laughs, reloads, blams some more. Something like that.[41]

Proulx also benefits from the current practice of viewing a novelist's writing less in terms of prose than in terms of individual sentences. Critics go through a novel half-consciously adding up the "good" ones, by which they mean the showy kind that can stand alone in the excerpt box, and if these attain a certain critical mass — the more famous the writer, the slighter the mass — the book is praised. (The ratio of good sentences to bad is not taken into account, which explains why some novelists are more than happy to discuss their work in terms of sentences instead of prose.[*]) Far from complaining about the incompatibility of form and content, Proulx's reviewers praise her sentences for having lives of their own. They "dance and coil, slither and pounce" (K. Francis Tanabe, *The Washington Post*), "every single sentence surprises and delights and just bowls you over," (Carolyn See, *The Washington Post*), a Proulx sentence "whistles and snaps" (Dan Cryer, *Newsday*).[42] In 1999 K. Francis Tanabe kicked off *The Washington Post*'s online discussion of Proulx's work by asking participants to join him in "choosing your favorite sentence(s) from any of the stories in *Close Range*."[43] Now, what reviewer in the old days would have expected people to have a favorite sentence from a work of prose fiction? A favorite passage, sure, a favorite line of dialogue, maybe, but a favorite *sentence*? You have to read a great novel more than once to realize how consistently good the prose is, because the first time around, and often even the second, you're too involved in the story to notice. John Skow raves of Proulx's language that "when it works, which is most of the time, it sweeps aside all ideas, her own and the reader's, and allows no response except banging the hands together."[44] Can such language really be said to be working?

[*] Typical is Vince Passaro's article "Dangerous Don DeLillo" (*The New York Times*, May 19, 1991), which contains fourteen references by both Passaro and DeLillo to sentences – "chiselled sentences," "lean sentences," pleasure in "the construction of sentences," a quote from *Mao II* in which a writer refers to himself as "a sentence maker," etcetera – and not one reference to prose. *The Atlantic Unbound* reported that Jonathan Franzen "longs to discuss sentences." I could go on.

Reviewers today often lapse into the style of the writer they are praising, so when reading about Proulx's work be prepared for a lot of bad taste, indifferent grammar and contrivedly "literary" expression:

> Birds, building materials and human body parts are equal grist to Ms. Proulx's language mill, which grinds brilliant prose out of them all. (Walter Kendrick, *The New York Times*) [45]

> [Proulx] grapples herself to her people with such authentic language that when poetry turns up, the grapple holds and they unforcedly elevate. (Richard Eder, *The New York Times*) [46]

Note how Eder scorns *ascend* for the transitive *elevate*; you can just imagine Proulx nodding in approval, and Skow banging his hands together.

And no discussion of Proulx is complete without the mention of poetry. Carolyn See, for example, tries to explain why the author of *Close Range* is "the best prose stylist working in English now, bar none,"[47] by positing a resemblance between the rhythm of her sentences and the poetry of Gerald Manley Hopkins. It is relevant to quote Connolly again:

> There is no reason why prose should not be poetical provided that the poetry in it is assimilated to the medium and that its rhythms follow the structure of prose and not of verse — it is the undisciplined, undigested, unassimilated poetry written often in unconscious blank verse and bearing no relation to the construction, if any, of the book, which has discredited "fine writing." [48]

Thomas Hardy, the only writer in English to achieve undisputed greatness as both novelist and poet, would have agreed with those sentiments. There was a time when most American critics would have agreed too; not for nothing did Thomas Wolfe's *Look Homeward, Angel* receive such a lukewarm reception back in 1929. If it were to come out today, of course, its very affectation would make it a shoo-in for the National Book Award, but at least attributes like "poetic" and "lyrical" would be justified:

> Once Daisy, yielding to the furtive cat-cruelty below her mild placidity, took him with her through the insane horrors of the scenic railway; they plunged bottomlessly from light into roaring blackness, and as his first yell ceased with a slackening of the car, rolled gently into a monstrous lighted gloom peopled with huge painted grotesques, the red maws of fiendish heads, the cunning appearances of death, nightmare, and madness ... Half-sensible, and purple with gasping terror, he came out finally into the warm and practical sunlight. [49]

This is a bit much perhaps, and after a few pages the unrelieved intensity of description proves only slightly less wearying than the grind of Proulx's "language mill." All the same it's a vivid scene, and but for *mild placidity* the words have been carefully chosen. The figures of speech all make sense (*cat-cruelty*, *practical sunlight*), each clause is good enough to stand on its own — and we still manage to see the fun-house ride through the eyes of a child and not an adult. For all his failings as a novelist, there is no denying that Thomas Wolfe possessed both a poet's originality of vision and the eloquence to put it on paper. Can the same be said for our work-driven friend?

EDGY PROSE

In one of his non-fiction essays Don DeLillo claims that
the prominence in television talk shows of the skinhead,
"with that pale stubble on his head,"

> has raised an unexpected image, that of the
> shorn European Jew filmed by Allied libera-
> tors. And we are helpless to break them apart.
> It is one more dread, one more victory of igno-
> rance. The bullyboy has consumed and incor-
> porated our memory of the victim without
> even realizing it. They are horribly locked in
> single bareface, the neo-Nazi and the death
> camp inmate, and this complex image col-
> lapses time and meaning and all sense of dis-
> tinctions. It is one more haunted message in
> the river of blur and glut, the painted stream
> that passes daily through our lives.[50]

Translation: Since the skinhead thugs on television and
the walking skeletons in Auschwitz newsreels all have
shorn heads, we have trouble keeping them apart in our
minds, and this makes it harder for us to distinguish
between the Nazis and their victims. Some ideas are
beneath comment. Suffice to assume that DeLillo,

despite that first person plural, doesn't consider himself incapable of seeing beyond the most trivial form of physical resemblance. He doesn't really believe you are either. He just wants to end his essay with a dramatic assertion, and he thinks that if he dresses it up in enough imagery — "the river of blur and glut, the painted stream" — he can make it seem true on a less demanding "literary" level. If you like this sort of thing, then you'll love DeLillo's novels. Just don't expect good prose. After all, this is a man who uses "river" and "stream" as synonyms.

Here is the oft-praised opener to *White Noise* (1985):

> The station wagons arrived at noon, a long shining line that coursed through the west campus. In single file they eased around the orange I-beam sculpture and moved toward the dormitories. The roofs of the station wagons were loaded down with carefully secured suitcases full of light and heavy clothing; with boxes of blankets, boots and shoes, stationery and books, sheets, pillows, quilts; with rolled-up rugs and sleeping bags, with bicycles, skis, rucksacks, English and Western saddles, inflated rafts. As cars slowed to a crawl and stopped, students sprang out and raced to the rear doors to begin removing the objects inside; the stereo sets, radios, personal computers; small refrigerators and table ranges; the cartons of phonograph records and cassettes; the hairdryers and styling irons; the tennis rackets, soccer balls, hockey and lacrosse sticks, bows and arrows; the controlled substances, the birth control pills and devices; the junk food still in shop-

ping bags — onion-and-garlic chips, nacho
thins, peanut creme patties, Waffelos and
Kabooms, fruit chews and toffee popcorn; the
Dum-Dum pops, the Mystic mints.[51]

You don't have to have read anything published after 1960
to know at once what you're in for: a tale of Life in
Consumerland, full of heavy irony, trite musing about
advertising and materialism, and long, long lists of consumer artifacts, all dedicated to the proposition that
America is a wasteland of stupefied shoppers. Critics like
to call this kind of thing "edgy" writing, though how an
edge can be discerned on either style or theme after fifty
years of blunting is anyone's guess. This will always be
foolproof subject matter for a novelist of limited gifts. If
you found the above shopping list witty, then DeLillo's
your man. If you complain that it's just dull, and that you
got the joke about a quarter of the way through, he can
always counter by saying, "Hey, I don't *make* the all-
inclusive, consumption-mad society, I just report on it."
You get the idea.

Of course the narrator, a professor called Jack
Gladney, can't actually *see* what's inside the students'
bags; he's just trying to be funny. So is there really a car-
avan of station wagons, or is that also a joke? How much
of that passage are we supposed to care about, or even to
bother visualizing? Such questions nag at the reader
throughout *White Noise*. We are no sooner introduced to
Jack and his wife than their conversation marks them as
impossible contrivances.

"It's the day of the station wagons."...
"It's not the station wagons I wanted to see.
What are the people like? Do the women wear

plaid skirts, cable-knit sweaters? Are the men
in hacking jackets? What's a hacking jacket?"[52]

No real person would utter those last two questions in
sequence. DeLillo's characters live in a middle-class
America that looks familiar, but they routinely talk and
act like visitors from another planet. This would be fine if
White Noise were simply a comedy, but it is not; it presents itself as a dead-on satire of the way we live now. The
American supermarket is described as a soothing place
where people go to satisfy deep emotional needs. (In an
interview after the novel's publication DeLillo elaborat-
ed on the theme by comparing supermarkets to church-
es.[53]) This sort of patronizing nonsense is typical of
Consumerland writers; someone should break the news to
them, since they've obviously never wondered why the
milk and bread are kept so far apart, that the average
shopper feels nothing in a supermarket but the strong
urge to get out again. DeLillo also continues a long intellectual tradition of exaggerating the effects of advertising. Here Steffie, the narrator's young daughter, talks in
her sleep.

> She uttered two clearly audible words, famil-
> iar and elusive at the same time, words that
> seemed to have a ritual meaning, part of a ver-
> bal spell or ecstatic chant.
>
> *Toyota Celica.*
>
> A long moment passed before I realized this
> was the name of an automobile. The truth
> only amazed me more. The utterance was
> beautiful and mysterious, gold-shot with
> looming wonder. It was like the name of an
> ancient power in the sky, tablet-carved in

> cuneiform.... Whatever its source, the utterance struck me with the impact of a moment of splendid transcendence.[54]

DeLillo has said that he wants to impart a sense of the "magic and dread" lurking in our consumer culture, but what a poor job he does of this! There is so little apparent wonder in the girl's words that only a metaphor drawn from recognizable human experience could induce us to share Jack's excitement. Instead we are told of an unnamed name carved on a tablet in the sky, and in cuneiform to boot. The effect of all this is so uninvolving, so downright silly, that even sympathetic readers tend to think that Jack is just trying to be funny again. It is left to real-life professors to set the record straight — in view not of the text itself (God forbid), but of what DeLillo has said elsewhere about how people allegedly use words to assuage a fear of death. In an essay appended to a recent issue of *White Noise* Cornel Bonca writes, "If we see Steffie's outburst as an example of the death-fear speaking *through* consumer jargon, then Jack's wondrous awe will strike us, strange as it may seem, as completely appropriate."[55] Fellow "DeLillo scholar" Paul Maltby concurs, assuring us that despite a common misconception the *Celica* passage is "not parodic"; we are meant to "listen in earnest" to this illustration of the power of names.[56] Good novelists, of course, make their readers listen in earnest to begin with. Far stranger things happen in Gogol's fiction, but we don't need academic intermediaries to tell us how to make them *seem* appropriate.

Even DeLillo's fans seem to have trouble accepting *White Noise* as fully felt. *The New York Times*' Christopher Lehmann-Haupt concludes that it is little more than "a vehicle for [DeLillo's] brilliant writing and gags,"[57] while implying that this is more than enough for any reader to demand. But is it really? And more to the point, is this kind of thing — to select another well-known passage — really brilliant writing?

> In the mass and variety of our purchases, in the sheer plenitude those crowded bags suggested, the weight and size and number, the familiar package designs and vivid lettering, the giant sizes, the family bargain packs with Day-Glo sale stickers, in the sense of replenishment we felt, the sense of well-being, the security and contentment these products brought to some snug home in our souls — it seemed we had achieved a fullness of being that is not known to people who need less, expect less, who plan their lives around lonely walks in the evening.[58]

Could the irony be any less subtle? And the tautology: "mass," "plenitude," "number"; "well-being," "contentment"! The clumsy echoes: "size," "sizes"; "familiar," "family"; "sense of," "sense of"; "well-being," "being"! I wouldn't put it past DeLillo's apologists to claim that this repetition is meant to underscore the superfluity of goods in the supermarket, but the fact remains that here, as in the *Celica* scene, the magical appeal of consumerism is described in prose that is merely flat and tiresome.

Most of DeLillo's thoughts, regardless of which character's mouth he stuffs them into, express themselves in strings of disjointed or elliptical statements. This must be what satisfies critics that they are in the presence of a challenging writer, but more often than not "the dry, shrivelled kernel," to borrow a line from Anne

Brontë, "scarcely compensates for the trouble of cracking the nut."[59] Here Jack Gladney is telling a woman why he gave his child the name Heinrich.

> "I thought it was forceful and impressive.... There's something about German names, the German language, German *things*. I don't know what it is exactly. It's just there. In the middle of it all is Hitler, of course."
>
> "He was on again last night."
>
> "He's always on. We couldn't have television without him."
>
> "They lost the war," she said. "How great could they be?"
>
> "A valid point. But it's not a question of greatness. It's not a question of good and evil. I don't know what it is. Look at it this way. Some people always wear a favorite color. Some people carry a gun. Some people put on a uniform and feel bigger, stronger, safer. It's in this area that my obsessions dwell."[60]

So Gladney thinks there is something forceful about German names. This is such a familiar idea that we naturally assume DeLillo is going to do more with it. Instead he gives us a *non sequitur* about Hitler and television, followed by a clumsy rehashing of the first point. If the narrator's obsessions dwell "in this area," shouldn't he be able to tell us something the rest of us don't know, something more than "Some people put on a uniform and feel bigger, stronger, safer"?

But let's go step by step through one of DeLillo's more serious attempts at philosophizing in *The Names* (1982).[61] This ploddingly realistic novel is set in Greece, and features as its protagonist an American expatriate called James. Though an intellectual obsessed with language, James cannot speak even enough Greek to tell his concierge Niko where he is going.

> In time I began to lie. I would tell him I was going to a place that had a name I could easily pronounce. What a simple, even elegant device this seemed. Let the nature of the place-name decide the place.

But James is *not* letting the nature of the name decide the place. He is merely letting the nature of the name decide the name. Simple, yes. Elegant? Of course not.

> But the lies began to worry me after a while.... There was something metaphysically disturbing about them. A grave misplacement.

Either something is disturbing or it isn't; the word "metaphysically" is there for no other purpose than to persuade readers that what follows will be over their heads. Just in case they miss the point they are told flat-out not to trust their common-sense:

> [The lies] were not simple but complex.

Now it is time to start putting over the central "idea."

> What was I tampering with, the human faith in naming, the lifelong system of images in Niko's brain? I was leaving behind in the person of the concierge an enormous discrepancy

> between my uttered journey and the actual
> movements I made in the external world, a
> four-thousand mile fiction, a deep lie.

But since Niko does not know where James is really going, no "discrepancy" is being left behind in him, and neither his "faith in naming" nor his "lifelong system of images" is being tampered with. Even if he *did* know the guest's true destination, he would merely conclude that he is being lied to. DeLillo knows this too of course, so he throws in the following:

> The lie was deeper in Greek than it would
> have been in English.

This may put any last doubts to rest for monolingual readers, but those of us who know that it's always easier to lie in a foreign language (or swear, or say we love someone) become more skeptical than ever. Of course, DeLillo has an answer ready.

> I knew this without knowing why.

So we've come full circle. The trivial issue of one man deceiving his concierge has gone from being puffed up into a grave metaphysical problem — i.e. one of universal human relevance — to being deflated into a personal issue that conveniently defies articulation. But then the puffing up starts again, as we are asked to ponder the significance of James' purely individual response to Greek sounds:

> Could reality be phonetic, a matter of gut-
> turals and dentals?

As so often with DeLillo's musings, the "conclusion" is phrased as a rhetorical question. "If this works for you, take it," he is saying, "but if you think it's silly, hey – maybe I do too." We can't even judge for ourselves whether reality is phonetic — whatever that means exactly — because DeLillo won't let us in on how James's lies sound in their exotic "gutturals and dentals." Clever, eh? There's just one problem: the only reason James is lying in the first place is in order to use words that are easy for an American to pronounce — words that are "phonetically" familiar.

I realize that these are to some extent questions of content, and that even great writers are rarely profound. But at least they sincerely believe what they're saying, and the reader can disagree while still deriving pleasure from the way they say it. I know, I know: *de gustibus* and all that. No doubt DeLillo's fans find "I knew this without knowing why" to be a marvelously eloquent way of putting things. They'd better, because these variations of the parental "because I say so" turn up often in his attempts at reasoning. We've already seen one of them:

> "There's something about German names...I
> don't know what it is exactly. It's just there."
> (*White Noise*)[62]

Here's something even more trite:

> What do you know about them?
> They weren't Greek.
> How do you know that?
> You see it right away. Faces, clothes, mannerisms.
> It's just there.
> (*The Names*)[63]

And this was quoted approvingly by a *Salon* reviewer:

> Time is supposed to pass, she thought. But
> maybe he is living in another state. It is a
> kind of time that is simply and overwhelm-
> ingly there. (*The Body Artist*)[64]

Now, one way that contemporary writers like to lower our expectations for their work is to claim that something as inadequate as language can never do justice to the complexity of what they're trying to say. Many readers fall for this too; it is precisely the clumsiness of "it's just there" that indicates to them the profundity behind it. (They don't need to know any more than that; it's the thought of the thought that counts.) Alas, DeLillo has unwisely gone on record as saying that for him, "writing is a concentrated form of thinking."[65] Which makes you wonder what the diluted form is like.

In fact, as the above examples indicate, DeLillo's characters do a lot less thinking than feeling; it just seems like thought because we are never made to feel anything ourselves. Descriptions of momentous sensations and portents are no sooner begun than they are left hanging in the air. In the following example Jack Gladney ponders all the clutter in his house:

> "Why do these possessions cast such sorrow-
> ful weight? There is a darkness attached to
> them, a foreboding. They make me wary not
> of personal failure and defeat but of some-
> thing more general, something large in scope
> and content."
> She came in with Wilder and set him down on
> the counter... [66]

This may be headily suggestive stuff for some readers, but the idea that a greater and truer reality exists behind the world of phenomena is as old as civilization itself. Shouldn't we expect a novelist, especially one billed as a thinker, to do more than muse that something "large in scope and content" attaches to personal possessions? This is the timid, sneaky vagueness of astrologers and palm-readers, and it turns up throughout DeLillo's novels. In *Underworld* (1997) a man's mouth fills with "the foretaste of massive inner shiftings";[67] another character senses "some essential streak of self";[68] the air has "the feel of some auspicious design";[69] and so on.

As with Proulx's writing, this is far duller in context than out of it, though it should be said in fairness that DeLillo's dullness often appears to be intentional. The inventory of luggage at the start of *White Noise* is far from the only passage in which he tries to bore us into laughing.

> "What do you want to do?" she said.
> "Whatever you want to do."
> "I want to do whatever's best for you."
> "What's best for me is to please you," I said.
> "I want to make you happy, Jack."
> "I'm happy when I'm pleasing you."
> "I just want to do what you want to do."
> "I want to do whatever's best for you."[70]

And so on. To anyone who calls that excruciating, DeLillo would probably respond, "That's my whole point! This is communication in Consumerland!" Note also how the exchange loses its logic halfway through; perhaps it was only written to be skimmed anyway. It's always the very novelists who scorn realism as the slavish recording of reality who believe that an incoherent world dictates incoherent writing.

But why should we bother with Consumerland fiction at all, if the effect of reading it is the same queasy fatigue we can get from an evening of channel-surfing? Do we need DeLillo for insight that rarely rises above the level of "some people put on a uniform and feel bigger"? Or do we need him for an ironic perspective that most of us acquired in childhood, when we first started sneering at commercials? It's not as if his themes haven't been tackled elsewhere, and in far better books. It would be cruel in this context to discuss Elias Canetti's theory of crowds, which Gladney/DeLillo seems to think is his own,[71] or to quote Robert Musil on anything, since there is more to think about in the first pages of *The Man Without Qualities* (1942) than in all of *White Noise*. But DeLillo looks small even next to more conventionally minded writers.

Take Balzac for example. He too was interested in what people wear and eat, in the furniture they use and the products they purchase, but unlike DeLillo he was able to show that what people own is, in translator Marion Crawford's words, "both an extension of personality and a molding force."[72] The following is worth comparing to the start of *White Noise*:

> [Lucien] saw around him exquisite studs on gleaming white shirts: his were russet-brown! All these elegant gentlemen had beautifully cut gloves while his were fit only for a policeman! One of them toyed with a handsome bejeweled cane, another's shirt had dainty gold cuff-links at the wrists...And another was drawing from his waistcoat pocket a

35

watch as flat as a five-franc piece and was keeping his eye on the time like a man who was too
early or too late for a rendezvous. At the sight
of these fascinating trifles which were something new to Lucien, he became aware of a
world in which the superfluous is indispensable, and he shuddered at the thought that he
needed enormous capital if he was to play his
part as a smart bachelor![73]

Both Jack Gladney and Lucien find themselves in "a world
in which the superfluous is indispensable," but instead of
giving us a lazy shopping list, with the patronizing implication that everything on it is just well-marketed junk,
Balzac makes us sense the attraction of "these fascinating
trifles"; he knew people too well to believe that they would
buy things they didn't want. And note how Lucien sees
around him a society of real human beings, each with individual tastes and traits, while Jack Gladney sees, or
claims to see, faceless students arriving at university at
the same time, in the same station-wagons, with the same
food in the trunk.

There's no who's-on-first drudgery in Balzac's dia-
logues either. Here the anti-hero of *Old Goriot* (1834) introduces himself:

"Hear me first, and you can talk after. I can tell
you my previous history in a couple of words.
Who am I? I'm Vautrin. What do I do? Whatever I
like. So let's get on."[74]

Vautrin goes on to sum up the hypocrisy of his age in an
effort to persuade Lucien to join him:

"Virtue, dear student, is not divisible. It either is, or isn't. We are told to do penance for our sins. A pretty system, isn't it, that quits you of a crime by an act of contrition? Seduce a woman so that you can get on to a higher rung on the social ladder; sow dissension among the children in a family; practice any of the infamies that are done daily in the home, in the pursuit of pleasure or self-interest — do you consider those to be acts of faith, hope and charity? Why do we give only two months in prison to a philanderer who in one night robs a child of half its fortune — and hard labor for life to a poor devil who steals a thousand-franc note with aggravating circumstances? Those are the laws for you! There's not a single article in them that doesn't touch absurdity. The gentleman with yellow gloves and yellow words has committed murders where no blood has been spilt. The blood has been *given*. The other man has opened a door with a crowbar! — and both are deeds of darkness!...You think there are absolutes in the world! Then disregard your fellow men, and just see how many loopholes there are that you can get through in the Code. At the bottom of every great fortune without apparent source, there's always some crime — a crime overlooked because it's been carried out respectably."[75]

Granted, this is only slightly more profound than DeLillo's observation that not all Europeans look like Greeks, but it is far better expressed — not in the

37

"pyrotechnic" way that makes today's critics stand up and cheer, but with the same effortless wit and energy that suffuse all of Balzac's best novels from start to finish. While DeLillo's characters sound uncannily like the author does in interviews, Balzac's all speak in unique voices; none of the several thousand characters in *The Human Comedy* sounds even remotely like Vautrin, for example. This is just one reason why Balzac is so much better than DeLillo at capturing a chaotic reality, even though he presents it (as DeLillo cannot) in a coherent form. Some may claim that we need contemporary fiction to address the unique realities of our time. How is it, then, that Vautrin's monologue is as relevant today as when it was written, while the strenuously topical *White Noise* has dated like an open box of cereal? Hardly had it gone into paperback than the station wagon bit the dust, television ratings began their long decline, and the Internet made all that ominous talk of radio waves sound as quaint as the scientific jargon in *Frankenstein*. You have to keep reminding yourself that the story isn't taking place in the 1970s.

DeLillo's publishers show the same sincerity in marketing his fiction that he shows in writing it. The dust-jacket of the hardback edition of *White Noise* intones: "Radio transmissions, sirens, ultrasonic and electronic waves — these omnipresent signals that buzz and hum all over America — both bewitch us and instill fear."[76] They do? "Like the ancient music of Pan, white noise pulses with life and at the same time signals death."[77] It does? With the critics' hype it is more difficult, as always, to distinguish between bad faith and bad taste. *White Noise* received the National Book Award in 1985. In *The New York Times* Jayne Anne Phillips wrote that

> [the narrator of *White Noise*] is one of the most
> ironic, intelligent, grimly funny voices yet to
> comment on life in present-day America. This
> is an America where no one is responsible or
> in control; all are receptors, receivers of stim-
> uli, consumers.[78]

Which sounds an awful lot like an America that Andy
Warhol began commenting on in the sixties, and in far
more coherent fashion to boot. Warhol even *wrote* better,
for God's sake. But postmodernism presupposes nothing
so much as the willing suspension of cultural literacy.

Most of *White Noise's* reviewers in 1985 hedged
their bets by praising DeLillo's intellect — or, my
favorite, his "analytic rigor" (Jay McInerney)[79] — while
offering no more than a phrase or two of textual evidence,
preferring instead to give away most of the novel's silly
plot. Phillips at least had the guts to give an example of
what she called DeLillo's "understanding and perception
of America's soundtrack."[80] Here Jack's colleague
Murray Suskind is expounding on the semiotics of —
what else? — the supermarket:

> "Everything is concealed in symbolism . . . The
> large doors slide open, they close unbidden.
> Energy waves, incident radiation . . . code
> words and ceremonial phrases. It is just a
> question of deciphering . . . Not that we would
> want to . . . This is not Tibet. . . . Tibetans try to
> see death for what it is. It is the end of attach-
> ment to things. This simple truth is hard to
> fathom. But once we stop denying death, we
> can proceed calmly to die . . . We don't have to

> cling to life artificially, or to death...We
> simply walk towards the sliding doors. Look
> how well-lighted everything is...sealed
> off...timeless...Another reason why I think
> of Tibet. Dying is an art in Tibet....Chants,
> numerology, horoscopes, recitations. Here we
> don't die, we shop. But the difference is less
> marked than you think."[81]

You couldn't make that any less coherent if you mixed
the sentences up in a hat and pulled them out again at
random. I hasten to add that Ms. Phillips made all those
ellipses herself, in a brave but futile attempt to isolate a
logical thought from the original mess. All the same, she
claimed that this passage constitutes strong evidence of
DeLillo's "understanding and perception." This is the
irony of Consumerland fiction: its fans are even more
helpless in the presence of authoritative posturing, and
even more terrified of saying, "I don't understand," than
the suburban shoppers they feel so superior to. The very
incoherence of DeLillo's writing recommends it to some.
"We listen intently," writes Lehmann-Haupt in praise of
White Noise, "trying to grasp what DeLillo means."[82] A
blurb on the first page of *The Names* raves that it is
"impossible to decipher fully."[83] These are selling points
in a dumbed-down nation; it is easier to wonder what
someone is trying to say, especially someone like this,
than to read Musil or Canetti and have to follow a progression of intelligent ideas.

Critics unite in calling DeLillo's work funny:
"absurdly comic...laugh-out-loud funny" (Michiko
Kakutani),[84] "grimly funny" (Jayne Anne Phillips),[85]
"tremendously funny" (*New Republic*)[86] and most agree
with Christopher Lehmann-Haupt that *White Noise* is

"one of his funniest."[87] But with a timidity worthy of
their idol they refuse to furnish examples of what they
find so amusing. I have a notion it's things like "Are the
men wearing hacking jackets? What's a hacking jacket?" but it would be unfair to assert this without evidence. Luckily for our purposes Mark Osteen, no less an
authority than President of the Don DeLillo Society,
has singled out a conversation in *White Noise* about the
word "entering" as one of the best bits of "sparkling dialogue" in a "very funny" book.[88] It is telling that the
same cultural establishment that never quite "got" the
British comic novel should split its sides at stuff like
this:

> "I will read," she said. "But I don't want you to
> choose anything that has men inside women,
> quote-quote, or men entering women. 'I
> entered her.' 'He entered me.' We're not lob-
> bies or elevators. 'I wanted him inside me,' as
> if he could crawl completely in, sign the regis-
> ter, sleep, eat, so forth. Can we agree on that?
> I don't care what these people do as long as
> they don't enter or get entered."
> "Agreed."
> "'I entered her and began to thrust.'"
> "I'm in total agreement," I said.
> "'Enter me, enter me, yes, yes.'"
> "Silly usage, absolutely."
> "'Insert yourself, Rex. I want you inside me,
> entering hard . . .'" [89]

And so on. Osteen would likely have groaned at that if it
had turned up in a television sit-com. The fuss he makes
over it in this context is a good example of how patheti-

cally grateful readers can be when they discover — lo and behold! — that a "literary" author is actually trying to entertain them for a change.

DeLillo's admirers call him "dangerous,"[90] but his reputation offers a far more devastating insight into American culture, and particularly our respect for authority figures, than his novels do. "If anyone has earned the right to bore us for our own good, it's Don DeLillo," writes *Salon's* Maria Russo.[91] "Since he is smarter than we are," intones John Leonard in the *New York Review of Books*, "trust him"[92] — something that never needed to be said of any truly smart writer in history. Then there's the more specifically postmodern belief, one often peddled by novelist-critics, and for obvious reasons, that intentions count for more than their execution: "*Underworld* may or may not be a great novel," says Martin Amis, "but there is no doubt that it renders DeLillo a great novelist."[93] And this is the same cultural elite that sees itself in the avant-garde tradition of irreverence, of taking nothing for granted! Imagine how André Breton would have reacted to this *Newsweek* report about a public reading of *The Body Artist* (2001):

> Jonathan Franzen came out to introduce Don DeLillo, the author of perfect sentences, paragraphs that equal poems...Had DeLillo heard such cheering?...DeLillo picked up from chapter two:
>
> > *"How completely strange it suddenly seemed that major corporations mass-produced breadcrumbs and packaged and sold them everywhere in the world and she looked at the breadcrumbs car-*

> ton *for the first true time, really seeing it*
> *and understanding what was in it, and*
> *it was breadcrumbs."*

[More perfect sentences from *A Body Artist* are quoted — BRM]

He read for 30 minutes. And then the fans came.... benign youngish men, nerdy, but not at all smarty-pants pretentious, kind of sweet.... As the line wound down, one DeLillo head said to the other, in a panic: "He's losing patience." In other words, maybe we shouldn't have gotten on line three different times with four books each time. Maybe, but he was gracious...[94]

Then I'll try to be more gracious myself, and concede that the man certainly seems smarter than his fans. And as far as I'm concerned, he can bore *them* all he wants.

MUSCULAR PROSE

The masculine counterpart to the ladies' prose poetry is a bold, Melvillean stiltedness, better known to readers of book reviews as "muscular prose." The acknowledged leader of this school is Cormac McCarthy, though it must be said that he once wrote in a very different style. *The Orchard Keeper* (1965), his debut novel, is a minor masterpiece of careful and restrained writing. An excerpt from the first page:

> Far down the blazing strip of concrete a small shapeless mass had emerged and was struggling toward him. It loomed steadily, weaving and grotesque like something seen through bad glass, gained briefly the form and solidity of a pickup truck, whipped past and receded into the same liquid shape by which it came. [95]

There's not a word too many in there, and although the tone is hardly conversational, the reader is addressed as the writer's equal, in a natural cadence and vocabulary. Note also how the figurative language ("like something seen through bad glass") is fresh and vivid without seeming to strain for originality.

44

Now read this from McCarthy's *The Crossing* (1994), the second part of his acclaimed Border Trilogy:

> He ate the last of the eggs and wiped the plate
> with the tortilla and ate the tortilla and
> drank the last of the coffee and wiped his
> mouth and looked up and thanked her.[96]

This is good example of what I call the *andelope*: a breathless string of simple declarative statements linked by the conjunction *and*. Like the "evocative" slide-show and the Consumerland shopping list, the andelope encourages skim-reading while keeping up the appearance of "literary" length and complexity. But like the slide-show (and unlike the shopping list), the andelope often clashes with the subject matter. It certainly does here, where the unpunctuated flow of words bears no relation to the methodical meal that is being described. Not for nothing do thriller writers save this kind of breathless syntax for climactic scenes of violence: "and his shout of fear came as a bloody gurgle and he died, and Wolff felt nothing...." (Ken Follett, *The Key to Rebecca*, 1980)[97]

And why does McCarthy repeat tortilla? When Hemingway writes, "small birds blew in the wind and the wind turned their feathers" ("In Another Country," 1927) he is, as David Lodge points out, using wind in two different senses, and creating two sharp images in the simplest way possible. McCarthy's second tortilla is only there, like the syntax, to draw attention to himself. For all the sentence tells us, it might as well be this:

> He ate the last of the eggs. He wiped his plate
> with the tortilla and ate it. He drank the last

of the coffee and wiped his mouth. He looked
up and thanked her.

Had McCarthy written that, critics would have reproached
him for his "workmanlike" prose. But the original is no
more informative, "evocative" or pleasing to the ear than
the second version, which can at least be read aloud in a
natural fashion. All the original does is say, "I express
myself differently from the man in the street, therefore I
am a writer."

And by his archaisms shall ye know him, for a
"muscular" novelist cannot write about our nation's
heroic past without slipping instinctively into the pseu-
do-Biblical style of *Moby Dick* — appropriately dumbed
down, of course. Take this example, from McCarthy's
Blood Meridian (1985):

> They caught up and set out each day in the
> dark before the day yet was and they ate cold
> meat and biscuit and made no fire.[98]

Even the Border Trilogy (*All the Pretty Horses*, *The
Crossing*, *Cities of the Plain*), which is set in the middle of
the twentieth century, is marked by formulations like
"and they would always be so and never be otherwise,"[99]
and "from whence there could be no way back forever." [100]

The reader is evidently meant to be carried along
on the stream of sonorous language. Reviewing *The
Crossing* for the *New York Times*, Robert Hass praised the
effect as follows:

> It is a matter of straight-on writing, a veering
> accumulation of compound sentences, stingi-
> ness with commas, and a witching repetition

> of words ... Once this style is established, firm,
> faintly hypnotic, the crispness and sinuous-
> ness of the sentences ... gather to a magic. [101]

The key word here is *accumulation*. Like Proulx and so many writers today, McCarthy relies more on barrages of hit-and-miss verbiage than on careful use of just the right words.

> While inside the vaulting of the ribs between
> his knees the darkly meated heart pumped of
> who's will and the blood pulsed and the bowels
> shifted in their massive blue convolutions of
> who's will and the stout thighbones and knee
> and cannon and the tendons like flaxen
> hawsers that drew and flexed and drew and
> flexed at their articulations of who's will all
> sheathed and muffled in the flesh and the
> hooves that stove wells in the morning
> groundmist and the head turning side to side
> and the great slavering keyboard of his teeth
> and the hot globes of his eyes where the world
> burned. (*All the Pretty Horses*)[102]

This sort of thing may get Hass's darkly meated heart pumping, but it's really just bad poetry reformatted to exploit the lenient standards of modern prose. The obscurity of *who's will*, which has an unfortunate Dr. Seussian ring to it, is meant to bully readers into thinking that the author's mind operates on a plane higher than their own — a plane where it isn't ridiculous to eulogize the shifts in a horse's bowels.

  And yet: it is ridiculous. As a fan of movie westerns, I refuse to quibble with the myth that a rugged landscape can bestow an epic significance on the lives of its

47

inhabitants. But as Conrad understood better than Melville, the novel is a fundamentally irreverent form; it tolerates epic language only when used with a selective touch. To record with the same majesty every aspect of a cowboy's life, from a knife-fight to his lunchtime burrito, is to create what can only be described as kitsch. Here we learn that out west, under a big hat, even a hangover is something special:

> [They] walked off in separate directions through the chaparral to stand spraddle-legged clutching their knees and vomiting. The browsing horses jerked their heads up. It was no sound they'd ever heard before. In the gray twilight those retchings seemed to echo like the calls of some rude provisional species loosed upon that waste. Something imperfect and malformed lodged in the heart of being. A thing smirking deep in the eyes of grace itself like a gorgon in an autumn pool. (*All the Pretty Horses*) [103]

It is a rare passage in a rare book that can make you look up, wherever you may be, and wonder if you are being subjected to a diabolically thorough *Candid Camera* prank. I can *just* go along with the idea that horses might mistake human retching for the call of wild animals. But "wild animals" isn't epic enough; McCarthy must blow smoke about "some rude provisional species," as if your average quadruped had table manners and a pension plan. Then he switches from the horses' perspective to the narrator's, though just what "something imperfect and malformed" refers to is unclear. The last half-sentence only deepens the confusion. Is the "thing smirking in the eyes of grace"

48

the same thing that is "lodged in the heart of being"? And what is a gorgon doing in a pool? Or is it peering into it? And why an *autumn* pool? I doubt if even McCarthy can explain any of this; he just likes the way it sounds.

But it is violence that shifts McCarthy's lyricism into high gear. This is from *Blood Meridian*:

> A rattling drove of arrows passed through the company and men tottered and dropped from their mounts. Horses were rearing and plunging and the mongol [sic] hordes swung up along their flanks and turned and rode full upon them with lances...some with nightmare faces painted on their breasts, riding down the unhorsed Saxons and spearing and clubbing them and leaping from their mounts with knives and running about on the ground with a peculiar bandylegged trot like creatures driven to alien forms of locomotion and stripping the clothes from the dead and seizing them up by the hair and passing their blades about the skulls of the living and the dead alike and snatching aloft the bloody wigs and hacking and chopping at the naked bodies, ripping off limbs, heads, gutting the strange white torsos and holding up great handfuls of viscera, genitals, some of the savages so slathered up with gore they might have rolled in it like dogs and some who fell upon the dying and sodomized them with loud cries to their fellows.[104]

I hasten to add that all this is dead serious. So where to start faulting such excess? With the overwrought effort to trick up the stalest scene in B-moviedom? With the chutzpah of comparing native Americans to the invaders of Europe? With those disgraceful last lines? None of this, mind you, can be defended as assuming the cowboys' own perspective, for the narrator of *Blood Meridian* is as omniscient as they come. Before the battle above, one Comanche is described as wearing the armor of a "spanish conquistador." (Unlike Saxon, "spanish" doesn't merit a capital "s".) This armor is "deeply dented with old blows of mace or saber done in another country by men whose very bones were dust."[105] The terror-stricken cowboys don't know that, nor do they need to, and since a dent is a dent, the information hardly helps us see things more clearly. So why explain who battered one man's armor, and where, and how long ago? Again: for the majestic ring of it. Sure, the action would be more exciting if seen through the eyes of the participants themselves, but the last thing Serious Literature wants to be is exciting.

All the same, we are dealing here with the conventional worldview of the Western novel, and with the same cast of characters: the quiet cowboys, the women who "like to see a man eat," the howling savages. There is certainly nothing new in McCarthy's philosophy, which exhausts itself in banal andelopes about death and fate.

> For God will not permit that we shall know what is to come. He is bound to no one that the world unfold just so upon its course and those who by some sorcery or by some dream might come to pierce the veil that lies so darkly over all that is before them may serve by just that vision to cause that God should wrench the world from its heading and set it upon another

> course altogether and then where stands the
> sorcerer? (*Cities of the Plain*) [106]

Try reading that passage out loud, and you'll realize why McCarthy is so averse to giving public readings.[107] His prose is unspeakable in every sense of the word.

There is also, as in most Western fiction, plenty of mythologizing about horses, the central myth being that they need us as much as we need them. If McCarthy had a more developed sense of humor it could be entertaining here too. Instead we get this sort of thing:

> [He] said that the souls of horses mirror the souls of men more closely than men suppose and that horses also love war. Men say they only learn this but he said that no creature can learn that which his heart has no shape to hold.... Lastly he said that he had seen the souls of horses and that it was a terrible thing to see. He said that it could be seen under certain circumstances attending the death of a horse because the horse shares a common soul and its separate life only forms it out of all horses and makes it mortal.... Finally John Grady asked him if it were not true that should all horses vanish from the face of the earth the soul of the horse would not also perish for there would be nothing out of which to replenish it but the old man only said that it was pointless to speak of there being no horses in the world for God would not permit such a thing. (*All the Pretty Horses*)[108]

The further we get from our cowboy past the loonier becomes the hippophilia we attribute to it. (I think it was Robert Graves who said that nothing marks the Koran more clearly as the product of a desert people than its lack of reference to camels; no one who grows up abusing animals for transport is likely to spend much time pondering their souls.) More to the point is the stiltedness with which the conversation is reproduced. The cowboys are supposed to be talking to the Mexican in Spanish, which is a stretch to begin with, but from the tone in which the conversation is set down you'd think it was ancient Hebrew. And if Grady were a believable teenager — hell, a believable *anyone* — he would ask just what a horse's soul looks like and why it's so terrible to behold, thereby satisfying our own curiosity. Instead he pursues a hypothetical point of equine theology; you half expect him to ask how many horses' souls can fit on the head of a pin.

The New York Times may praise McCarthy's "realistic dialogue," but his characters' direct speech is no less hard to swallow. Here is a Mexican woman in *All the Pretty Horses*. (Needless to say, literature this serious has no need for quotation marks.)

> The political tragedy in Spain was rehearsed in full dress twenty years earlier on Mexican soil. For those with eyes to see. Nothing was the same and yet everything. In the Spaniard's heart is a great yearning for freedom, but only his own. A great love of truth and honor in all its forms, but not in its substance. And a deep conviction that nothing can be proven except that it be made to bleed. Virgins, bulls, men. Ultimately, God himself.[109]

And here is a border-town pimp in *Cities of the Plain*:

> Your kind cannot bear that the world be ordi-
> nary. That it contain nothing save what stand
> before one. But the Mexican world is a world of
> adornment only and underneath it is very
> plain indeed. While your world — he passed the
> blade back and forth like a shuttle through a
> loom — your world totters upon an unspoken
> labyrinth of questions.[110]

Believable speech may be low on McCarthy's list of priorities, but he fills whole pages with untranslated
Spanish conversation, which he knows, and this invali-
dates the comparison to Tolstoy's French, that most of
his readers cannot understand. Like the archaisms, the
missing quotation marks, and the gorgon in the pool, the
Spanish is meant to make his writing seem more difficult
than it is.

A. O. Scott may be right in saying that novels like
All the Pretty Horses offer "men living late in the history of
civilization a consoling picture of their own inner wild-
ness,"[111] but it would be naïve to think that this doesn't
appeal to women too. Critic Sara Mosle praises the "sexy
subtext" of a passage on horse-training in *Cities of the
Plain*, adding: "If cowboys can do this for horses, imagine
what they can do for women."[112] McCarthy also benefits
from the fact that middle-class snobs, for all their love of
cowboy hokum, would no sooner be caught with a "genre"
Western than with a comic book. Otherwise they'd be
defecting in droves to Louis L'Amour, who delivers the
same myths more skillfully. In this passage the epony-
mous hero of *Hondo* (1953) has just asked a woman not to
feed his dog.

She had the feeling that he was a man that lived in continual expectation of trouble, never reaching for it, yet always and forever prepared. Her eyes dropped to the worn holster and the polished butt of the Colt. Both had seen service, and the service of wear and use, not merely of years.

"Oh, I think I understand. You don't want him to get in the habit of taking food from anyone but you. Well, I'll just fix it and you can hand it to him."

"No, ma'am. I don't feed him either."

When her eyes showed their doubt, he said, "Sam's independent. He doesn't need anybody. I want him to stay that way. It's a good way."

He helped himself to another piece of meat, to more potatoes and gravy.

"But everyone needs someone."

"Yes, ma'am." Hondo continued eating. "Too bad, isn't it?"[113]

No andelopes, no pseudo-Joycean tomfoolery with punctuation — just crisp, believable dialogue. Vittoro, the novel's Apache character, is drawn with respect and compassion; the contrast to *Blood Meridian*'s howling necrophiles is sharp but not surprising. Born in Sioux country of solid frontier pedigree, complete with a scalped ancestor, L'Amour had as little need for a newcomer's overconformism as he did for absurd cowboy worship. Though no philosopher by any means, he was at least as much of a thinker as McCarthy:

No man knows the hour of his ending, nor can he choose the place or the manner of his

> going. To each it is given to die proudly, to die
> well, and this is, indeed, the final measure of
> the man.[114]

But too easily understood, no? Too — how you say? — *work-manlike*. Let's make it more evocative, more compelling:

> And to no man is it given to know the hour of
> his death nor is it given to him to choose the
> place of his death or the manner of his death
> but rather to die proudly and to die well. And
> it cannot be otherwise that this is indeed the
> final measure of the man and it will always
> be so.

Fortunately for millions of readers around the world, L'Amour was less interested in winning prizes than in telling a good story: "That's the way I'd like to be remembered," he told an interviewer, "as a storyteller."[115] So of course the critics dismiss *Hondo* as pulp, just as many book-reviewers once regarded *Treasure Island* as fit only for children. The cultural establishment likes to reserve its accolades for those who take themselves most seriously. But how many critics will care to be reminded of Cormac McCarthy in twenty years? The smart money's on the storyteller.

For the moment, of course, he is doing very well indeed. *All the Pretty Horses* received the National Book Award in 1992. "Not until now," the judges wrote in their fatuous citation, "has the unhuman world been given its own holy canon."[116] What a difference a little archaizing makes! McCarthy's "holy canon" offers nothing more than the conventional belief that horses, like dogs, serve us well enough to merit humane treatment — unlike the rest of the animal kingdom. (No one ever sees a cow's soul.)

Not all McCarthy's novels have been quite so well received, but his place at the forefront of contemporary literature is never questioned. Entire newsletters and websites are devoted to his work, and the Cormac McCarthy Society still meets annually in El Paso, where the writer lives, to discuss such appropriately kitschy topics as "Sacred Violence" and "the Morality of Blood." No one else takes his philosophizing very seriously, for which we should perhaps be grateful, and reviewers generally gloss over the episodic plots. Shelby Foote informs us that the real hero of McCarthy's work "is the English language — or perhaps I should say the American language."[117] *The New York Times* says he "puts most other American writers to shame."[118] *The Village Voice* calls him "a master stylist, perhaps without equal in American letters."[119]

Comparisons with Faulkner are especially common,[120] though Robert Hass assures us that *The Crossing* will remind us of Shakespeare and Conrad too.[121] Just as Eder speaks Proulxian when reviewing *Close Range*, so does Hass slip into High Cowboy Mandarin in praise of Cormac:

> The boys travel through this world, tipping their hats, saying "yessir" and "nosir" and "si" and "es verdad" and "claro" to all its potential malice, its half-mad philosophers, as the world washes over and around them, and the brothers themselves come to be as much arrested by the gesture of the quest as the old are by their stores of bitter wisdom and the other travelers, in the middle of life, in various stages of the arc between innocence and experience, by whatever impulses have placed them on the road.[122]

But the vagueness of that tribute probably annoys McCarthy, who prides himself on the way he tackles "issues of life and death" head on. In interviews he presents himself as a man's man with no time for pansified intellectuals — a literary version, if you will, of Dave Thomas, the smugly parochial old-timer in the Wendy's commercials. It would be both unfair and a little too charitable to suggest that this is just a pose. When Cormac says of Marcel Proust and Henry James, "I don't understand them. To me, that's not literature,"[123] I have a sinking feeling he's telling the truth.

SPARE PROSE

Anyone who doubts the declining literacy of book reviews need only consider how the gabbiest of all prose styles is invariably praised as "lean," "spare," even "minimalist." I am referring, of course, to the Paul Auster School of Writing.

> It was dark in the room when he woke up. Quinn could not be sure how much time had passed — whether it was the night of that day or the night of the next. It was even possible, he thought, that it was not night at all. Perhaps it was merely dark inside the room, and outside, beyond the window, the sun was shining. For several moments he considered getting up and going to the window to see, but then he decided that it did not matter. If it was not night now, he thought, then night would come later. That was certain, and whether he looked out of the window or not, the answer would be the same. On the other hand, if it was in fact night here in New York, then surely the sun was shining somewhere else. In China, for example, it was no doubt mid-afternoon, and the rice-farmers were

58

mopping sweat from their brows. Night and day were no more than relative terms; they did not refer to an absolute condition. At any given moment it was always both. The only reason we did not know it was because we could not be in two places at the same time. (*City of Glass*)[124]

This could have been said in half as many words, but then we readers might feel emboldened to ask why it needed to be said at all. (Who ever thought of night and day as "an absolute condition" anyway?) The flat, laborious wordiness signals that this is avant-garde stuff, to miss the point of which would put us on the level of the morons who booed *Le Sacre du Printemps*. But what is the point? Is the passage meant to be banal, in order to trap philistines into complaining about it, leaving the cognoscenti to relish the postmodern irony of it all? Or is there really some hidden significance to this time-zone business? The point, as Auster's fans will tell you, is that there can be no clear answer to such questions: fiction like *City of Glass* urges us to embrace the intriguing ambiguities that fall outside the framework of the conventional novel. All interpretations of the above passage are allowed, even encouraged — except of course for the most obvious one: that Auster is simply wasting our time.

Here is another example of what passes for intellectual content in his fiction:

"Remember what happened to the father of our country. He chopped down the cherry tree, and then he said to his father, 'I cannot tell a lie.' Soon thereafter, he threw the coin across the river. These two stories are crucial events in

American history. George Washington chopped down the tree and then he threw away the money. Do you understand? He was telling us an essential truth. Namely, that money doesn't grow on trees.... That tree was the Tree of Life, and it would have made us immune to death.... But the father of our country knew his duty. He could not do otherwise. That is the meaning of the phrase, 'Life is a bowl of cherries.'" (*City of Glass*)[125]

It's always risky to identify a novelist's thoughts with his characters', but the prevalence of these free-associations makes it hard not to conclude that Auster finds them either amusing or profound. Here's Willy, a character in *Timbuktu* (1999):

"It's all flit and fume, my boy, a bellyful of wind.... Grant me swizzle sticks and dental floss, Dentyne gum and honey dip doughnuts. Delete Dana Andrews and Dixie Dugan, then throw in Damon Runyan and demon rum for good measure. Forget Pall Malls and shopping malls, Milton Berle and Burle Ives, Ivory Soap and Aunt Jemima pancake mix. I don't need them, do I?"[126]

Nor do we. There's a stale point in there about stimulus overload in Consumerland, one that will undoubtedly thrill the DeLillo crowd, but did the author really have to drag us through a tiresome parlor game to make it? Lawrence Sterne's characters ramble on too, and manage to say equally little of importance, but at least they're fun to listen to.

Here's Fogg in Auster's *Moon Palace* (1989):

> One thought kept giving way to another, spi-
> raling into ever larger masses of connected-
> ness. The idea of voyaging into the unknown,
> for example, and the parallels between
> Columbus and the astronauts. The discovery
> of America as a failure to reach China;
> Chinese food and my empty stomach;
> thought, as in food for thought, and the head
> as a palace of dreams. I would think: the
> Apollo Project; Apollo, the god of music...It
> went on and on like that, and the more I
> opened myself to these secret correspondenc-
> es, the closer I felt to understanding some
> fundamental truth about the world. I was
> going mad, perhaps, but I nevertheless felt a
> tremendous power surging through me, a
> gnostic joy that penetrated deep into the
> heart of things. Then, very suddenly, as sud-
> denly as I had gained this power, I lost it.[127]

That talk of "secret" correspondences and "gnostic joy" is
meant to make more trusting readers think there must
be some insight here which they are too dim to grasp. To
forestall accusations of childishness from the rest of us
the narrator is careful to add, "I was going mad, perhaps,"
just as he adds the "bellyful of wind" disclaimer in
Timbuktu. Like DeLillo, Auster knows that equivocation
is *sine qua non*. As long as he keeps his intentions under
wraps at all times, he is free to counter all criticism of
plot, style and character by invoking the catch-all slogan
engraved on postmodernism's coat of arms: "But that's
the whole *point*!"

What gives Auster away is his weakness for erudite facetiousness. In passages like these it becomes so obvious what Nabokovian effect he is aiming for, and so obvious that he can't pull it off, that the whole house of cards comes tumbling down.

> When I met Kitty Wu, she called me by several other names... Foggy, for example, which was used only on special occasions, and Cyrano, which developed for reasons that will become clear later. Had Uncle Victor lived to meet her, I'm sure he would have appreciated that Marco, in his own small way, had at last set foot in China. (*Moon Palace*)[128]

By falling in love with a Chinese woman, the narrator can perhaps be said to have "discovered" China, though God knows that's awful enough, but *set foot* in it? It is no mean feat to be precious and clumsy at the same time, but Auster pulls it off on almost every page. Some more examples:

> [At school the name] Fogg lent itself to a host of spontaneous mutilations: Fag and Frog, for example, along with countless meteorological references: Snowball Head, Slush Man, Drizzle Mouth. (*Moon Palace*)[129]

> ... a new tonality had crept into the bronchial music — something tight and flinty and percussive... (*Timbuktu*) [130]

> Was Mr. Bones an angel trapped in the flesh of a dog? Willy thought so.... How else to inter-

pret the celestial pun that echoed in his mind
night and day? To decode the message, all you
had to do was hold it up to a mirror. Could
anything be more obvious? Just turn around
the letters of the word *dog*, and what did you
have? The truth, that's what. (*Timbuktu*)[131]

Nobody's perfect. But why should we forgive someone for
trying to pass off a schoolboy anagram as "a celestial pun,"
or "snowball" as a meteorological reference, or "tonality"
as a synonym for "tone," when he himself is trying so hard
to draw attention to his fancy-pants language? Nor are
these excerpts improved by being read in context. (The
bullies who terrorize the young Fogg only stumble onto
"Shit Face" after a careful progression through Marco
Polo, Polo Shirt and Shirt Face.) Even harder to stomach
is the way Auster abuses philosophical terms.

According to him, [the name Marco Stanley
Fogg] proved that travel was in my blood, that
life would carry me to places where no man had
ever been before. Marco, naturally enough,
was for Marco Polo, the first European to visit
China; Stanley was for the American journal-
ist who had tracked down Dr. Livingstone "in
the heart of darkest Africa"; and Fogg was for
Phileas, the man who had stormed around the
globe in less than three months....In the short
run, Victor's nominalism helped me to survive
the difficult first few weeks in my new school.
(*Moon Palace*)[132]

This is aimed at people who are just educated enough to
know that nominalism has something to do with names,

and ignorant enough to believe that such words lend philosophical significance to a trite story. In fact nominalism says that just because words exist for generalities like humanity doesn't mean that these generalities exist. What does that have to do with Victor's talk?

Name-dropping is another characteristic of Auster's prose; historical and literary figures, titles of books, etc, are bandied about in an attempt to impress and flatter the reader:

> The songs struck me as a revelation — filled with humor and spirit, a boisterous form of mayhem that mocked everything from politics to love. Victor's lyrics had a jaunty, dittylike flavor to them, but the underlying tone was almost Swiftian in its effect. Spike Jones meets Schopenhauer, if such a thing is possible. (*Moon Palace*)[133]

One example of these fascinating lyrics would have obviated all that prattle, but Auster couldn't be bothered to think one up. Like DeLillo, he baldly asserts what he cannot make us feel. Another example:

> Once, for example, we stopped an elevator between floors, and as the angry tenants of the building yelled and pounded because of the delay, I pulled down Kitty's jeans and panties and brought her to an orgasm with my tongue. Another time, we did it on the bathroom floor at a party, locking the door behind us and paying no attention to the people lined up in the hall, waiting their turn to use the

> john. It was erotic mysticism, a secret reli-
> gion restricted to just two members. (*Moon
> Palace*) [134]

A better writer would give that last sentence the build-up
it needs, but Auster isn't interested enough in real life to
do the job; if the paragraph were a car it would carry the
bumper sticker *I'd rather be making celestial puns*. A man
brings a woman to orgasm with his tongue, they do "it" on
a bathroom floor — so what? None of this dead prose tells
us why an act that is usually restricted to two members
should in this case constitute "erotic mysticism, a secret
religion." Or does having sex with people in hearing range
make everything more secret? Lest anyone claim that
minimalism is all about leaving things to the reader's
imagination, note how Auster feels the need to explain
not only why the angry tenants yelled and pounded for
the elevator — because of the delay! — but also why the
party-goers were lined up outside the bathroom: they
wanted to use it!

This brings us to the main hallmark of Auster's
style, and of much contemporary prose in general.

> His nostrils were turned into suction tubes,
> sniffing up scents in the way a vacuum clean-
> er inhales bits of glass, and there were times
> — many times, in fact — when Willy marveled
> that the sidewalk did not crack apart from
> the force and fury of Mr. Bones' snout
> work.... Normally the most obliging of crea-
> tures, the dog would grow stubborn, distract-
> ed, seem to forget his master entirely, and if
> Willy happened to tug on the leash before Mr.

> Bones was ready to move on, before he had
> ingested the full savor of the turd or urine pud-
> dle under his scrutiny, he would plant his legs
> to resist the yank, and so unbudgeable did he
> become, so firmly did he anchor himself to the
> spot, that Willy often wondered if there wasn't
> a sac hidden somewhere in his paws that could
> secrete glue on command. (*Timbuktu*)[135]

Never mind the cute flights of fancy (glue on paws, etc)
and the clumsy combination of "ingested" and "savor,"
which inadvertently implies that the dog is eating. More
remarkable is the way that almost every phrase or attribute is followed by one that either says the same thing or
adds too little meaning to warrant the inclusion of both:
"suction tubes, sniffing"; "vacuum cleaner...inhales";
"there were times — many times, in fact"; "force and
fury"; "distracted, seem to forget his master entirely";
"before Mr. Bones was ready to move on, before he had
ingested the full savor"; "so unbudgeable did he become,
so firmly did he anchor himself to the spot," etc. Swing
the hammer often enough, and you're bound to hit the
nail on the head sometime — or so Auster seems to think.

> His body burst into dozens of small pieces,
> and fragments of his corpse were found...
> (*Leviathan*)[136]

> Blue can only surmise what the case is not. To
> say what it is, however, is completely beyond
> him. (*Ghosts*)[137]

> My father was tight; my mother was extrava-
> gant. She spent; he didn't. (*Hand to Mouth*)[138]

Inexpressible desires, intangible needs, and
unarticulated longings all passed through the
money box and came out as real things, palpable objects you could hold in your hand. (*Hand
to Mouth*)[139]

Still and all, Mr. Bones was a dog. From the
tip of his tail to the end of his snout, he was a
pure example of *Canis familiaris*, and whatever
divine presence he might have harbored within his skin, he was first and foremost the
thing he appeared to be. Mr. Bow Wow,
Monsieur Woof Woof, Sir Cur. (*Timbuktu*) [140]

This sort of thing is everywhere, and yet the relative
shortness of his sentences has always fooled critics into
believing that he never wastes a word. Michiko Kakutani
attributes to him a "writerly obsession with compression
and concision"[141] — and this in a review of *Hand to Mouth*,
by far his most repetitive book. *The Washington Post*'s
Dennis Drabelle writes, "Auster's prose is always eco-
nomical — clipped, precise, the last word in gnomic control,"[142] which looks like something Auster might have
written himself.

The Manhattan provenance and glacial pace of his
novels give the creator of Monsieur Woof Woof a certain
cachet in continental Europe, where his translators presumably take the fall for the quality of the prose. Not
that he is unknown in the English-speaking world. *Kirkus
Reviews* claims that he is "quickly becoming our preemi-
nent novelist of ideas."[143] He has also received the Morton
Dauwen Zabel Award from the American Academy of Arts
and Letters. (Why he hasn't yet received the National
Book Award I cannot imagine.) The same libraries that

can't get rid of old books fast enough are happy to lavish a good, in the sense of approximate, foot-and-a-half of shelf-space on his novels, which are festooned with raves from both sides of the Atlantic. London's *Sunday Telegraph* calls him "a genius of a novelist," while *The Village Voice* marvels at how a "slim volume" like *Moon Palace* (a paltry 307 pages) can "bear a burden of such philosophical weight."[144]

Now, if the British want to put Auster up there with Dickens, and the folks at *The Village Voice* have tumbled to the gnostic connections between Apollo and the Apollo Project, that's their business. But there's no excuse for praising the man's "spare" style (*Telegraph*), his "brisk, precise" writing (*The New York Times*), his "economy, precision" (*Publishers Weekly*) and his "straightforward, almost invisible prose" (*Village Voice*). [145] Either these critics have never read Isherwood, Maugham or any other masters of straightforward English, or they are consciously serving what Budd Schulberg once called "the grinding of gears and the crap." You decide which is more likely.

Of course, neither Auster nor any of the other writers featured in this book has received only rave reviews. But even their worst books, the ones well below the contemporary "literary" average — and that's saying something — are treated with respect. Let's take Jim Shepard's critique in *The New York Times* of Auster's *Timbuktu* (1999), a novel about which the kindest thing that can be said is that it is an improvement over his cant-filled memoir *Hand to Mouth* (1997). To his credit, Shepard notes the unpleasant cuteness of Auster's style, quoting this sentence as an example:

> The little fellow howled with laughter, and
> even though the thrust of Mr. Bones's tongue

> eventually made him lose his balance, the
> rough-and-tumble Tiger thought it was the
> funniest thing that ever happened to him, and
> he went on laughing under the barrage of the
> dog's kisses...[146]

But since Auster is a Serious Writer, Shepard has to accentuate the positive. The following, he writes, is one of the "periodic flashes of gorgeous prose" in *Timbuktu*:

> [The word Tucson evoked in the dog] the scent
> of juniper leaves and sagebrush, the sudden,
> unearthly plenitude of the vacant air.[147]

What novelist, having assumed the olfactory perspective of a canine, would think it more important to remind us that air is vacant than to drop a single word on just how those desert plants smell? Not that the first phrase doesn't have a pleasant slickness to it — *this Father's Day, give him the scent of juniper leaves and sagebrush* — but "gorgeous prose"? Maybe our nation's book-reviewers are just more generous than I am, but keep in mind how selective their generosity is. No one scours thrillers or romance novels in search of a decent line to praise, though I dare say there isn't a "genre" writer in the country who can't match the quality of that Auster quote every dozen pages or so. When it comes to non-"serious" fiction the Sentence Cult is forgotten; prose is treated as an indivisible whole, and no punches are pulled. Even a mild-mannered critic like Michiko Kakutani can feel safe mocking a Jackie Collins novel in the "yeah baby" lingo of Austin Powers.[148]

But back to "literary" fiction. As we saw with McCarthy, today's prize-winners are often likened to great dead writers, though never in a way that would make readers more interested in the latter. Metaphors of consanguinity are often belabored (Rick Moody is Cheever's "true heir, the next generation" — A. M. Homes[149]) until someone comes along to tell us that the new guy is even better (Moody is "funnier" than Cheever — Janet Burroway[150]). This nonsense serves the myth that literature is doing just fine, which in turn serves to legitimize a cultural establishment that has done more to discourage reading than all the TV networks put together. (The parallel to the old Soviet slogan "Stalin is the Lenin of today" is no coincidence.) It's only natural, then, to see Auster routinely likened to Samuel Beckett, though the two men's styles have virtually nothing in common. Here is a passage from *Malone Dies* (1951):

> I feel it is my duty to say that it is never light in this place, never really light. The light is there, outside the air sparkles, the granite wall glitters with all its mica, the light is against my window, but it does not come through. So that here all bathes, I will not say in shadow, nor even in half-shadow, but in a kind of leaden light that makes no shadow, so that it is hard to say from what direction it comes, for it seems to come from all directions at once, and with equal force. I am convinced for example that at the present moment it is as bright under my bed as it is under the ceiling, which admittedly is not saying much, but I need say no more....In a word there seems to be the light of the outer world, of those who know the sun and moon emerge at such an hour and at such another

plunge again below the surface, and who rely on this, and who know that clouds are always to be expected but sooner or later always pass away, and mine.... The noises too, cries, steps, doors, murmurs, cease for whole days, their days. Then that silence of which, knowing what I know, I shall merely say that there is nothing, how shall I say, nothing negative about it. And softly my little space starts to throb again.[151]

Here we have a man describing the emptiest of surroundings in a way that manages to be precise, vivid and interesting. He talks compulsively but not frivolously, repeating words without repeating himself. There is sadness here — "for whole days, their days" is a poignant line — and subtle humor too: "which admittedly is not saying much, but I need say no more." That last sentence in the passage is one of those piercingly poetic lines that came far too easily to Beckett for him to feel the need to draw attention to them. Nothing is taking place here in the usual sense, and yet we read on; our impulse to find out what will happen next is replaced by an impulse to find out where Malone's thinking will lead him.

Now go back, if you will, to the excerpt from *City of Glass* quoted at the beginning of this section. Two hundred flat, lifeless words, and what do they tell us? That it's hard to tell the time without looking out a window or checking a timepiece, and that the earth is round. The very reference to China in this context feels stale, though perhaps it's a sophomoric homage to *Ulysses*. ("What an unearthly hour I suppose they're just getting up in China now," etc.) For all I know, Auster has as deep and sincere an affection for Beckett's work as he keeps telling interviewers. But this is not how he *writes*; he writes as if he has just flipped through *Malone Dies*, found it dull and repetitive, and concluded that the deliberate use of dullness and repetition is a brilliant literary device.

It is from Jorge Luis Borges, on the other hand, that Auster borrows both his favorite allegories (detective work, biographical research) and his favorite theme: the impossibility of ever really *knowing* anything. But unlike Borges, Auster does not convey the sort of fun that makes intellectual exercise worthwhile after all. The gnostic correspondences between "Chinese food" and "food for thought"; dog spelled backwards is god — this is philosophical writing?

Of course, this banality is precisely what makes Auster so suited to modern reading habits. Whole pages can be skimmed with impunity. He creates a dog that understands English perfectly, only to tell you that it likes to sniff excrement. He christens his hero Marco Stanley Fogg, a name portending lots of onomastic exposition and tales of playground cruelty, and then spends pages making good on the threat. A man counts his books (why?) and finds there are precisely 1492 of them, and his nephew is going to a certain university in New York City. "A propitious number, I think, since it evokes...."[152] Go on. Take a wild guess.

GENERIC LITERARY PROSE

A thriller must thrill or it is worthless; this is as true now as it ever was. Today's "literary" novel, on the other hand, need only evince a few quotable passages to be guaranteed at least a lukewarm review. It is no surprise, therefore, that the "literary" camp now attracts a type of writer who, under different circumstances, would never have strayed from the safest crime-novel formulae, and that so many critically acclaimed novels today are really mediocre "genre" stories told in an amalgam of trendy stylistic tics. What unites these writers and sets them off from the Proulxs and DeLillos is the determinedly slow tempo of their prose. They seem to know that in leaner and livelier form their courtroom dramas, geisha memoirs and horse-whisperer romances would not be taken seriously, and that it is precisely the lack of genre-ish suspense that elevates them to the status of prize-worthy "tales of loss and redemption."

One of the most successful of these writers is David Guterson, who in 1996 was named by the tony literary journal *Granta* as one of America's twenty best young novelists. The following passage is from *Snow Falling on Cedars* (1994), which won the PEN/Faulkner and spent over a year on the *New York Times* bestseller list.

He didn't like very many people anymore or very many things, either. He preferred not to be this way, but there it was, he was like that. His cynicism — a veteran's cynicism — was a thing that disturbed him all the time…It was not even a thing you could explain to anybody, why it was that everything was folly. People appeared enormously foolish to him. He understood that they were only cavities full of jelly and strings and liquids. He had seen the insides of jaggedly ripped-open dead people. He knew, for instance, what brains looked like spilling out of somebody's head. In the context of this, much of what went on in normal life seemed wholly and disturbingly ridiculous…He sensed [people's] need to extend sympathy to him, and this irritated him even more. The arm was a grim enough thing without that, and he felt sure it was entirely disgusting. He could repel people if he chose by wearing to class a short-sleeved shirt that revealed the scar tissue on his stump. He never did this, however. He didn't exactly want to *repel* people. Anyway, he had this view of things — that most human activity was utter folly, his own included, and that his existence in the world made others nervous. He could not help but possess this unhappy perspective, no matter how much he might not want it. It was his and he suffered from it numbly.[153]

I apologize for the length of that excerpt, but it takes more than a few sentences to demonstrate the repetitive sluggishness of Guterson's prose. Michael Crichton could have given us the same stock character of the Alienated Veteran in one of those thumbnail descriptions he's always getting slammed for, while making sure that Ishmael exhibited at least one memorable trait or experience. Guterson, on the other hand, is content to stretch out a flat, stereotypical description as far as possible.

The word "thing" is used to add bulk. *You could not explain to anybody why everything was folly* becomes "It was not a thing you could explain to anybody, why it was that everything was folly"; *His cynicism disturbed him* becomes "His cynicism...was a thing that disturbed him"; *he believed that* becomes "he had this view of things — that." There is plenty of unnecessary emphasis, the classic sign of a writer who lacks confidence: "*enormously* foolish," "*wholly* ... ridiculous," "*entirely* disgusting." There are sentences that seem to serve no purpose at all:

> He could repel people if he chose by wearing to class a short-sleeved shirt that revealed the scar tissue on his stump. He never did this, however. He didn't exactly want to *repel* people. Anyway ...

Almost every thought is echoed:

> He preferred not to be this way, but there it was, he was like that ... He could not help but possess this unhappy perspective, no matter how much he might not want it.

> ... everything was folly. People appeared enormously foolish to him ... In the context of this, much of what went on in normal life seemed wholly and disturbingly ridicu-

louss... Anyway, he had this view of things —
that most human activity was utter folly...

You could study this passage all day, and the whole novel
for that matter, and find no trace of a flair for words. But
luckily for Guterson many readers, including the folks at
Granta, are willing to buy into the scam that anything
this dull must be Serious and therefore Fine and therefore Beautiful Writing.

Like Cormac McCarthy (to whom he is often compared), Guterson thinks it more important to sound literary than to make sense. This is the highly touted opening
to *East of the Mountains* (1998):

> On the night he had appointed his last among
> the living, Dr. Ben Givens did not dream, for
> his sleep was restless and visited by phantoms
> who guarded the portal to the world of dreams
> by speaking relentlessly of this world. They
> spoke of his wife — now dead — and of his
> daughter, of silent canyons where he had hunt-
> ed birds, of august peaks he had once ascended,
> of apples newly plucked from trees, and of
> vineyards in the foothills of the Apennines.
> They spoke of rows of campanino apples near
> Monte Della Torraccia; they spoke of cherry
> trees on river slopes and of pear blossoms in
> May sunlight.[154]

Now, if the doctor's sleep was visited by phantoms — "visited," mind you, not interrupted — then surely he was
dreaming after all? Or were the phantoms keeping him
awake? But isn't "restless sleep" still sleep? The answer, of
course, is that it doesn't matter one way or the other.

Guterson is just swinging a pocket watch in front of our eyes. "You're in professional hands," he's saying, "for only a Serious Writer would express himself so sonorously. Now read on, and remember, the mood's the thing."

What follows is a succession of images, none of which is even remotely fresh or vivid. By the end of the third sentence, with its cherry trees, pear blossoms and still more apples, the sheer accumulation of phrases is supposed to fool the reader into thinking that a lyrical effect has been created. The ruse is a little too obvious here. Proulx would have drawn the line at something as stale as "august peaks," especially in an opening paragraph. (She would also have avoided the clumsy echo of "restless" and "relentlessly.")

But if you note the last two words in "apples newly plucked from trees" you will see that Guterson is not trying to speed his readers along. On the contrary: a slow tempo is as vital to his pseudo-lyrical effects as a fast one is to Proulx's. What would otherwise be sprightly sentences are turned into mournful shuffles through the use of tautology. "Anything I said was a blunder, a *faux pas*,"[155] "a clash of sound, discordant,"[156] "She could see that he was angry, that he was holding it in, not exposing his rage,"[157] "Wyman was gay, a homosexual,"[158] and so on.

And this brings us, now that we've discussed the slide-show, the shopping list and the andelope, to the last of the four main forms of today's dumbed-down long sentence, namely the chant: a concatenation of uninspired phrases set to an elegiac cadence.

> They rode back all day to the Columbia, tra-
> versed it on the Colockum Ferry, and at dusk
> came to their orchard tired, on empty stom-
> achs, their hats tipped back, to walk the hors-

> es between the rows of trees in a silent kind of
> processional, and Aidan ran his hands over
> limbs as he passed them with his horse behind
> him, the limbs trembling in the wake of his
> passing, and on, then, to the barn.[159]

Note the lexicological speed-bumps: "a silent kind of pro-cessional" for "a silent processional," "in the wake of his passing" for "in his wake." The very reference to "limbs trembling" behind Aidan's back (limbs of trees that is; "branches" would have been clearer but too prosaic) is there purely for sound and rhythm. Granted, everything is botched by "on, then, to the barn" — but you get the principle. And never let it be said that this stuff doesn't work. James Marcus, one of the in-house critics at Amazon.com, praised the above excerpt for offering read-ers "miniature lessons in patience and perception."[160]

On the positive side, Guterson has more of a sto-rytelling instinct than many novelists today. Beneath all the verbal rubble in *Cedars* is a good murder mystery crying out be heard — feebly, perhaps, but still loud enough for *The New York Times* to have denied the book its usual non-"genre" bonus of a second review. Guterson also knows that he has no gift for figurative language; outbursts like "a labyrinth of runners as intricate as a network of arteries feeding"[161] are mercifully rare. As a result he sinks below mediocrity as rarely as he rises above it. Only the sex scenes are laughably bad.

> "Have you ever done this before?" he whis-
> pered.
> "Never," answered Hatsue. "You're my
> only."

The head of his penis found the place it
wanted. For a moment he waited there,
poised, and kissed her — he took her lower lip
between his lips and gently held it there. Then
with his hands he pulled her to him and at the
same time entered her so that she felt his
scrotum slap against her skin. Her entire
body felt the rightness of it, her entire body
was seized to it. Hatsue arched her shoulder
blades — her breasts pressed themselves
against his chest — and a slow shudder ran
through her.

"It's right," she remembered whispering. "It
feels so right, Kabuo."

"*Tadaima aware ga wakatta*," he had
answered. "*I understand just now the deepest
beauty.*" [162]

If Jackie Collins had written that, reviewers would have
had a field day with "You're my only," the searching
penis, the shudder's slow run. Thanks to that scrotum
slap, which makes you wonder just what Hatsue's body
felt the rightness of, the passage fails even on a Harlequin
Romance level. But critics gamely overlook the whole
mess, because by this point in the book Guterson has
already established himself as a Serious Writer — mainly
through length and somberness, but also through all
those Japanese words. In fact, what Kabuo is saying here
translates as "Now I understand *pity*," a mood-killer if
ever there was one. This error, still uncorrected after
umpteen reprintings, seems to rest on Guterson's misun-
derstanding of *mono no aware*, an aesthetic concept we'll
return to later. Suffice to say that his Japanese makes

about as much sense as Auster's philosophical terms.* Critics don't mind of course, as long as there are lots of unintelligible words in italics. ("The Philistine likes a little obvious recondity," as Baron Corvo once noted.[163]) *Cedars'* "exhaustive list of acknowledgments" was enough to convince *The New York Times* that "Guterson has done his homework."[164]

Almost every fourth amateur reviewer on Amazon.com complains about the repetitiveness of, as one wag refers to it, *Sleep Falling on Readers. Kirkus Reviews*, on the other hand, called the 345-page novel "compact as haiku," while *The New York Times* praised Guterson's "finely wrought and flawless writing."[165] The novel is now required reading in college English classes; perhaps this very moment a professor is reverently chalking "you're my only" on a blackboard. Some students even have to read Guterson in history class, in order to learn about the internment of Japanese-Americans in World War II. So much for *Farewell to Manzanar*, I suppose — another good book displaced from the canon by a bad one.

The Serious Writers' Club is a bit like the Mafia; once the critics "make" you, you're in for life, and the worst you'll ever hear is that your new book is not quite as hauntingly evocative as your old one. *East of the Mountains*, Guterson's tale of a dying man finding peace during a journey into rural Washington, thus got a pre-dictably respectful reception when it appeared in 1998. While slogging through it I remembered a far better novel

---

* In *Cedars* the Japanese immigrants constantly refer to Americans as whites or *hakujin*. In fact, the Japanese do not view the world in our color categories, but divide it into Japanese and non-Japanese (*gaijin*, a word which Japanese businessmen in the US will occasionally use to describe us locals). This is why it rings so false when a Japanese mother in *Cedars* warns her daughter against consorting with white people (page 64); a Japanese of that generation would have been more horrified to see her daughter bring a Korean or Chinese home.

with a comparable theme: Shiga Naoya's *A Dark Night's Passing* (*Anyakoro*, 1937). The hero, a writer named Kensaku, is followed from a joyless bachelorhood into an equally joyless marriage. After the death of his child he withdraws to a mountain temple. A strenuous climb with a group of younger men leaves him exhausted on the side of the mountain, where he falls asleep. The excursion ultimately brings him close to death (the book ends with his fate in doubt), but not before giving him the tranquility he has been seeking. The novel is shot through with a strange sadness; to read it is to understand what Japanese really mean by *mono no aware* or "the pity of things" — in other words, how both the good and the bad, the beautiful and the ugly, convey the sorrow of human existence.[166] The passage in which Kensaku wakes on the slope overlooking the ocean shows how a sharp eye and concise prose can create, even in translation, an effect that is both vivid and moving:

> When he opened his eyes again, the green around him had begun to show in the light of early dawn. The stars, though fewer now, were still there. The sky was soft blue — the color of kindness, he thought. The mist below had dispersed, and there were lights here and there in the villages at the foot of the mountain.... The big light that went on and off was surely from the lighthouse at Mihonoseki. The bay, as still as a lake, remained in the shadow of the mountain, but the sea outside had already taken on a grayish hue. All aspects of the scene changed rapidly with dawn's hurried progress. When he turned around, he saw the mountaintop outlined

against a swelling mass of orange light that became more and more intense; then the orange began to fade and everything around him became clearer. The wild grass grew shorter here than it did down below; and in its midst were large wild asparagus, standing singly and far apart from each other, their flowers dotting the landscape near and far.... A little bird flew out chattering, and like a pebble tossed in the air drew a sharp arc and dropped back into the grass.[167]

It's no coincidence that Shiga also wrote the classic "At Kinosaki" (1917), an autobiographical piece in which he describes his regret at accidentally killing a lizard with a stone.[168] To write well about nature requires a poetic sensibility that can't be faked. If you prefer to read books by a man who brags to interviewers, "I make recreation out of taking the lives of small birds,"[169] then be my guest. Just don't be surprised if all you get is a lesson in patience.

CONCLUSION

At the 1999 National Book Awards ceremony Oprah Winfrey told of calling Toni Morrison to say she had had to puzzle repeatedly over many of the latter's sentences. According to Oprah, Morrison's reply was: "That, my dear, is called reading."[170] Sorry, my dear Toni, but it's actually called bad writing. Great prose isn't always easy but it's always lucid; no one of Oprah's intelligence ever had to puzzle over what Joseph Conrad was trying to say in a particular sentence. This doesn't stop the talk-show host from quoting her friend's words with approval. In similar fashion an amateur reviewer on Amazon admits to having had trouble with David Guterson's short stories: "The fault is largely mine. I had been reading so many escape novels that I wasn't in shape to contend with stories full of real thought written in challenging style."[171]

This is what the cultural elite wants us to believe: if our writers make no sense, or bore us to tears, that can only mean that we aren't worthy of them. Bill Goldstein, an editor at *The New York Times Book Review*, wrote an article in July 2000 blaming the proliferation of unread bestsellers on readers who bite off more "intellectually intimidating" fare than they can chew.[172] Vince Passaro, writing for *Harper's* in 1999, attributed the unpopularity of new short fiction primarily to the fact that it is "smart" and "intellectual," in contrast (he claimed) to the short story of Hemingway's day.[173] Passaro named Rick Moody as a young talent to watch for, and offered this excerpt from "perhaps the best thing he's written," a short story called "Demonology" (1996):

> They came in twos and threes, dressed in the fashionable Disney costumes of the year, Lion King, Pocahontas, Beauty and the Beast, or in the costumes of televised superheroes, Protean, shape-shifting, thus arrayed, in twos and threes, complaining it was too hot with the mask on, *Hey, I'm really hot!*, lugging those orange plastic buckets, bartering, haggling with one another, *Gimme your Smarties, please?* as their parents tarried behind, grownups following after, grownups bantering about the schools, or about movies, about local sports, about their marriages, about the difficulties of long marriages; kids sprinting up the next driveway, kids decked out as demons or superheroes or dinosaurs or as advertisements for our multinational entertainment providers, beating back the restless souls of the dead, in search of sweets.[174]

By the third line you realize you're back in Consumerland. (Moody says he was "utterly blown away" by *White Noise*.[175]) Far from evincing any challenging content, unless you count those feeble digs at Disney, this sentence — half DeLilloesque shopping list, half Gutersonian chant — offers a good example of how little concentration is required by modern "literary" prose. You don't need to remember how it began in order to finish it; after all, Moody doesn't seem clear on who is "beating back the restless souls of the dead" either. (The metaphorical verb implies more awareness of the dead than can be attributed to either the excited children or their chattering parents.) You don't even need to take note of each word, because everything comes around twice anyway: "Protean, *shape-shifting*; in twos and threes... *in twos and threes*;" "complaining it was too hot with the mask on, *Hey, I'm really hot!*"; "as their parents tarried behind, *grownups following after*"; "in the costumes of televised superheroes, *kids decked out... as superheroes*"; etcetera. But none of this can hide Moody's tin ear (*"Hey, I'm really hot!"*), his unfamiliarity with the world of children (who haggle after they get home, and over less humdrum treats) and the absence of sharp or memorable detail.

All Passaro would say to justify quoting that passage was that it combines "autobiography, story, social commentary, and the irony to see them all as a single source of pain."[176] (I think I got the pain part.) This is a typical example of the American critic's aversion to discussing style at length. The implication is always the same: "If you can't see why that's great writing, I won't waste my time trying to explain." This must succeed in bullying some people, or all the purveyors of what Paul Fussell calls the "second-rate pretentious"[177] would have been forced to find honest work long ago. Still, I'll bet that for every three readers who finished that *Harper's* article, at least two did so with a mental note to avoid contemporary short fiction like the plague. Even a nation brainwashed to equate artsiness with art knows when its eyelids are drooping.

People like Passaro, of course, tend to think that anyone indifferent to the latest "smart" authors must be vegetating in front of the television, or at best silently mouthing through a Tom Clancy thriller. The truth is that a lot of us are perfectly happy with literature written before we were born — and why shouldn't we be? The notion that contemporary fiction possesses greater relevance for us because it talks of the Internet or supermodels or familiar brand names is ridiculous. We can see ourselves reflected more clearly in Balzac's Parisians than in a modern American who goes into raptures when his daughter says "Toyota Celica" in her sleep. This is not to say that traditional realism is the only valid approach to fiction. But today's Serious Writers fail even on their own postmodern terms. They urge us to move beyond our old-fashioned preoccupation with content and plot, to focus on form instead — and then they subject us to the least expressive form, the least expressive *sentences*, in the history of the American novel. When Don DeLillo describes a man's walk as "a sort of explanatory shuffle, a comment on the literature of shuffles,"[178] I feel nothing; the wordplay is just too insincere, too patently meaningless. But when Nabokov talks of midges "continuously darning the air in one spot,"[179] or the "square echo" of a car door slamming,[180] I feel what Philip Larkin hoped readers of his poetry would feel: "Yes, I've never thought of it that way, but that's how it is."[181] The pleasure that accompanies this sensation is almost addictive; for many, myself included, it's the most important reason to read both poetry and prose.

Older fiction is also fast becoming the only place left to experience the power of unaffected English. In this scene from Saul Bellow's *The Victim* (1947), a man meets a woman at a Fourth of July picnic:

> He saw her running in the woman's race, her
> arms close to her sides. She was among the

stragglers and stopped and walked off the field, laughing and wiping her face and throat with a handkerchief of the same material as her silk summer dress. Leventhal was standing near her brother. She came up to them and said, "Well, I *used* to be able to run when I was smaller." That she was not accustomed to thinking of herself as a woman, and a beautiful woman, made Leventhal feel very tender toward her. She was in his mind when he watched the contestants in the three-legged race hobbling over the meadow. He noticed one in particular, a man with red hair who struggled forward, angry with his partner, as though the race were a pain and a humiliation which he could wipe out only by winning. "What a difference," Leventhal said to himself. "What a difference in people."[182]

Scenes that show why a character falls in love are rarely convincing in novels. This one works perfectly, and with none of the "evocative" metaphor hunting or postmodern snickering that tends to accompany such scenes today. The syntax is simple but not unnaturally terse, a point worth emphasizing to those who think that the only alternative to contemporary writerliness is the plodding style of Raymond Carver. Bellow's verbal restraint makes the repetition of "what a difference" all the more touching. The entire novel is marked by the same quiet brilliance. As Christopher Isherwood once said to Cyril Connolly, talent doesn't manifest itself in a writer's affectation, but "in the exactness of his observation [and] the justice of his situations."[183]

It's easy to despair of ever seeing a return to that

kind of prose, especially with the cultural elite doing such a quietly efficient job of maintaining the *status quo*. (Rick Moody received an O. Henry Award for "Demonology" in 1997, whereupon he was made an O. Henry juror himself. And so it goes.) But the paper chain of mediocrity would perpetuate itself anyway. Clumsy writing begets clumsy thought, which begets even clumsier writing. The only way out is for the rest of us to look back to a time when authors had more to say than, "I'm a writer!" — when the novel wasn't just a three-hundred page caption for the photograph on the inside jacket. Many readers, of course, are already doing just that. Sales of classic novels have increased in the last five years, and small publishers are springing up to re-issue long-forgotten books.

The American literary press is faced with a clear choice. It can continue plugging unreadable new books until the last advertiser jumps ship, and the last of the stand-alone book-review sections is discontinued — as *The Boston Globe*'s was in 2001 — or it can start promoting the kind of novels that will get more Americans reading again. A good strategy would be to show that intellectual content can be reconciled with a vigorous, fast-moving plot, as in Budd Schulberg's novel *What Makes Sammy Run?* (1941) or John O'Hara's *Appointment in Samarra* (1934). Not that we have to stick to American writers. Patrick Hamilton's *Hangover Square* (1941) and Roy Fuller's *The Second Curtain* (1953) are British psychological thrillers written in careful, unaffectedly poetic prose; both could appeal to a wide readership here. By the same token, many of the adults who enjoy Harry Potter would be even happier with the *Gormenghast* trilogy (1946-1959) if they only knew about it, and suspense fans would be surprised to find how readable William Godwin's *Caleb*

Williams (1794) is. Americans should also be encouraged to overcome their growing aversion to translated fiction. If *The New York Times* can lavish two reviews on an American man's geisha memoirs — like we needed another Pearl Buck to whiten Asia for us — then surely it can spare a few inches for Enchi Fumiko's heartrending novel *The Waiting Years* (1957), or Mori Ogai's love story *Wild Geese* (1913).

Feel free to disparage these choices, but can anyone outside the publishing industry claim that the mere fact of a novel's newness should entitle it to more of our attention? Many readers wrestle with only one bad book before concluding that they are too dumb to enjoy anything "challenging." Their first experience with literature shouldn't have to end, for lack of better advice, on the third page of something like *Underworld*. At the very least, the critics can start toning down their hyperbole. How better to keep young people from reading than to invoke the names of great writers in praise of some windy new mediocrity every week? How better to discourage clear and honest self-expression than to call Annie Proulx, as Carolyn See did in *The Washington Post*, "the best prose stylist working in English now, bar none"? [184]

Whatever happens, the old American scorn for pretension is bound to re-assert itself some day, and dear God, let it be soon. In the meantime, I'll be reading the kind of books that Cormac McCarthy doesn't understand.

EPILOGUE

The Response to "A Reader's Manifesto"

THE RESPONSE TO "A READER'S MANIFESTO"

"Boy, are you in trouble," wrote a man who had enjoyed the magazine version of "A Reader's Manifesto," and he was only one of many who urged me to prepare for stern retribution. It was melodramatic, perhaps, but in a way that is worth paying attention to. Anyone who wonders why *The New York Times Book Review* is forced to shed a page or two every few years needs to realize that many Americans regard our cultural establishment as something akin to Orwell's Ministry of Truth. Having said that, I should make clear that the international response to the essay was overwhelmingly favorable. Only days after the July/August issue of *The Atlantic Monthly* went on sale in late June 2001, *The Wall Street Journal* devoted an editorial to the essay, and *The L.A. Examiner, The Observer, The Columbus Dispatch, The Albuquerque Tribune, The Arkansas Democrat-Gazette, The Sunday Times* and *The Times of London* all ran supportive articles in the course of the summer.[185] Jonathan Yardley wrote a full-length article in *The Washington Post* agreeing with the Manifesto, though re-reading it today — this is how spoiled I've become — I can't help noticing how carefully he refrains from praising it.[186] *The Australian Financial Review* carried the entire essay in two installments in

August,[187] inspiring critic Peter Holbrook to launch what he called a "Myersian" attack on novelist Peter Carey in the Sydney newspaper *The Australian* a few weeks afterward.[188] Even Cairo's *Al-Ahram Weekly* came down on my side. "I find myself," wrote columnist Mursi Saad El-Din, "in complete agreement with Mr. Myers."[189]

Not everyone felt the same way, of course. On July 16 *The Los Angeles Times* ran a lengthy feature on the Manifesto that included some negative remarks from critics and editors.[190] But oddly enough, no attempt at rebuttal was published until over a month after the essay's appearance. The position of the U.S. literary establishment seems to have been, for a while at least, that it was beneath notice. This is how Michael Dirda, of *The Washington Post Book World*, answered a reader's query in an online discussion on June 28:

> I've been sent the "Reader's Manifesto" article, but have only skimmed it. Most of the writers the author goes after are, in fact, people I admire: Proulx, McCarthy, DeLillo, Auster. I'm told it's pretty well done, however. But then, it seems to me that every decade or so we have an attack like this...No one will remember this article in a year, but people will be reading Proulx, McCarthy *et al* for a long, long time. [191]

A week later more people logged on to discuss the Manifesto, and again Dirda said he had only glanced at it.[192] The following week someone else asked if he had read it. His patience clearly wearing thin, he gave a revealing answer:

Didn't read it, probably won't. I don't agree
with the premise at all.[193]

A British reporter based in New York told me in July that
though her friends were talking about the essay, she
could find no one in the literary establishment who was
familiar with it. *The Los Angeles Times*' Mary McNamara
seems to have had the same problem:

> Other editors, agents and critics haven't read
> the essay, or simply "skimmed it," finding
> nothing new or remarkable in the tract. . . . Don
> Lee, editor of *Ploughshares*, a magazine of con-
> temporary fiction, who had not yet read
> Myers's piece [said] "Ten years ago the com-
> plaints were about minimalism. So now it's
> pretension. Not surprising."[194]

Now, the literary press announces a must-read novel
every week, chews over an Oprah choice every month, and
falls at the feet of two or three prize-winners a year. Can
anyone really have believed that because Tom Wolfe
raised some complaints about contemporary fiction in a
Harper's essay in 1989[195] — and on entirely different
grounds — the appearance of "A Reader's Manifesto" was
too routine an event to merit attention?

If the strategy was to ignore me in the hope that
readers would follow suit, it didn't work. By late July
various online forums were debating the essay, English
professors were assigning it for the fall semester, and
Amazon.com was reporting that customers who bought
books by Budd Schulberg were also buying books by
Shiga Naoya. When I visited *The Atlantic Monthly*'s offices

in Boston I was told that no one could remember having received such a broad and positive response to any article. There were seven supportive letters and e-mails for every critical one — a ratio that the magazine, for reasons I would love to see it own up to, inverted in what it actually chose to print. Mail came addressed to me from across the U.S. and from as far away as Portugal and Australia; the youngest writer was seventeen, the oldest ninety-eight. One American lady wrote to tell me that the mention of my name had brought her creative-writing teacher to the verge of angry tears. In short, I feel confident in claiming that mine was the first piece of literary criticism in American history to receive more attention from the public than from the cultural elite.

But in mid-July I began hearing a rumor that Steve Wasserman, editor of *The Los Angeles Times Book Review*, was looking for someone big and famous to put me in my place. When "Why Great Literature Contains Everything But a Clear Answer" finally appeared on July 29 it was under the name of Lee Siegel, a frequent contributor to the newspaper. A last-minute replacement? Perhaps; it is hard to read the piece and not conclude that it was written in haste. (And printed in haste too, with some sections directly on top of others, rendering much of it illegible; *The L.A. Examiner* promptly ran a story under the headline: "LAT Botches Attack On 'A Reader's Manifesto.'"[196]) There were also attempts at rebuttal in articles from Meghan O'Rourke at *Slate* (July 27), John Mark Eberhart at *The Kansas City Star*, who wrote a two-part article (July 29 and August 5), Bob Pohl at *The Buffalo News* (August 5) and Laura Miller at *Salon* (August 16).[197] *The New York Times Book Review* continued to ignore the Manifesto until well after the relevant issue of *The Atlantic Monthly* had ended its two-month run, when Judith Shulevitz launched a curiously parochial attack on it in her column "The Close Reader." (September 9).[198] Since these articles go over a lot of the same ground, as do some isolated remarks made by other critics and novelists, I think it is best to deal with each of the main arguments in turn. The amateur online book-reviewers who disagreed with me will find most of their complaints addressed here too.

DEFENDING DIFFICULTY

In schoolbook essay style I had put the crux of my argument at the end of the introduction, where everyone could expect to find it:

> If the new dispensation were to revive good "Mandarin" writing — to use the term coined by the British critic Cyril Connolly for the prose of Virginia Woolf and James Joyce — then I would be the last to complain. But what we are getting instead is a remarkably crude form of affectation: a prose so repetitive, so elementary in its syntax, and so numbing in its overuse of wordplay that it often demands less concentration than the average "genre" novel. Even today's obscurity is easy — the sort of gibberish that stops all thought dead in its tracks. The best way to demonstrate this in the space at hand is to take a look at some of the most highly acclaimed styles of contemporary writing.

And throughout the essay I used textual examples to prove "how little concentration is required by modern 'literary' prose." I lamented the easy syntax of the modern long sentence. I pointed out the banality of DeLillo's shopping lists and the skim-friendliness of Proulx's slide-shows. As if the reference to Joyce and Woolf weren't enough to reveal my own inclinations, I also drew attention to McCarthy's dismissal of Proust and James, noted how far Auster falls short of Borges, made an approving reference to Conrad, and contrasted the facile chanting of Rick Moody with excerpts from Bellow and Nabokov. I ended with a declaration to sit out the current malaise in literature by reading the work of James and Proust. Not once did I reproach anyone's prose with difficulty or complexity.

But just as the priests who fell foul of the Inquisition were all heretics, anyone who attacks the American literary establishment today simply *has* to be a philistine; no other explanation is possible. The most common way of rebutting the Manifesto was therefore not to rebut it at all, but to misrepresent it as a plea for lowbrow writing. This is the novelist T.C. Boyle, responding to a show of interest in the essay by contributors to his online message board:

> The author of this particular article seems to be making a case for philistinism....He seems to think that all novels should be written in the sort of prose employed by newspaper obituary writers or those inspired few who compose ingredient lists for mayonnaise jars.[199]

The critic Richard Eder made the following remark about me to *The Los Angeles Times*:

> This guy seems to think that if it's easy to
> read, it's good. Which is ridiculous.[200]

Indeed it is, and the ease with which such nonsense could
be discredited proved too tempting for *Slate*'s Meghan
O'Rourke, who called her attempt at rebuttal "Unfair
Sentences: The Case for Difficult Books."

> [Myers] attacks contemporary fiction for
> being...self-consciously difficult....Myers'
> dislike of writing that is self-consciously
> about ideas or language reflects an essential
> distrust of difficulty....The danger of Myers'
> irritation is self-evident: It implies we need-
> n't ever challenge ourselves as readers. [201]

According to *The Kansas City Star*'s John Mark Eberhart,
I jeered at book-reviewers for loving "beautiful diction
and clever syntax."[202] Michael Dirda's refusal to read the
Manifesto did not prevent him from asserting that I
attacked Proulx for writing "fine sentences."[203] Lee
Siegel claimed I dismissed "complicated syntax" for what
I saw as its "essential emptiness,"[204] which was an odd
thing to say, considering that my own syntax is a lot
more complicated than his. *Newsday*'s Dan Cryer, who
like Eder had received a critical mention in my piece,
wrote the following to *The Atlantic*:

> Poor B. R. Myers. The man simply can't fath-
> om writing that deviates from the norm
> established by Strunk and White....While
> hewing to the straightforward is good advice
> for undergraduates, writers of talent know

how to create and exploit whole universes of
expression beyond this narrow range.[205]*

All this would have been legitimate rhetoric if anyone
had taken the trouble to argue that what I saw as simple
and ugly prose was in fact complex and elegant. But no
one did this. Instead the Defenders of Difficulty proceed-
ed from the very assumptions I had set out to disprove.
O'Rourke:

> At the heart of Myers' screed is...a notion
> that story trumps style, or it ought to...In
> the first [story] camp, you've got, say,
> Trollope and Theodore Dreiser. In the other,
> you've got Flaubert and Joyce. We could divide
> many of today's fiction writers into these
> camps: On the side of story, there'd be John
> Irving, Amy Tan, Norman Mailer, and Stephen
> King, among others. On the side of sentence, or
> style, there'd be Thomas Pynchon, David
> Foster Wallace, Rick Moody, Jayne Anne
> Phillips, Bret Easton Ellis, and so on. But these
> categories are crude and reductive.[206]

As if any part of my "screed," let alone the heart of it, had
demanded that story trump style; as if I had not used the
introduction to mock precisely this division of literature
into story-telling versus form-oriented fiction. Note how
O'Rourke puts Rick Moody and friends in the company of
Flaubert and Joyce, as if this were something all sensible
people could agree on, then fills the "story" camp with an

---

* Cryer was gracious enough to acknowledge that when it came to
McCarthy I was right, whereas he and many of his colleagues had been
fooled. Interestingly enough, *The Atlantic Monthly* chose to delete that
part.

only slightly less bizarre mix of writers, and finally dismisses both these self-created categories as "crude and reductive." I used to wonder how book reviewers could be so impressed by the intellectual content of DeLillo's fiction. Now I'm beginning to understand.

Resorting to a more brazen misrepresentation of my views, Siegel claimed that I disliked the very writers I had praised in the Manifesto:

> Myers... associates any kind of complex writing about unquantifiable inner experience — for example, Woolf, Faulkner, Conrad, Joyce — with abstraction and pretentiousnesss...[Myers] really believes that Americans are too stupid to read complicated prose and that what Americans really want and deserve are action movies in book form.[207]

I also received some hate-mail in this vein. Someone I'll call Elmer wrote, "Don't have the balls to take on Joyce, do you?... You're a Phillistine [sic]. Grow up." Gerald Howard, a publishing executive who has edited DeLillo and Auster, referred to my essay in a letter to *The Atlantic Monthly* as "B. R. Myers' blast of sort of smart but definitely annoying literary philistinism."[208] None of these people, by the way, seemed to mind Cormac McCarthy's statement that Proust's work is "not literature."

And *Salon*'s book editor Laura Miller took it upon herself to give "anyone who hasn't read the original essay" this breezy summary:

> Some commentators, like Siegal [sic], insist that the essay is a demand that literary prose

be "easy" to read; others describe it as a complaint about the decline of plot. Actually, it's about both.[209]

Which was news to me.

Not that all this came out of thin air. Much was made of my lead-off declaration, which I will gladly renew here, that I would rather read Stephen King than the latest prize-winning novel. In circles where books are read for cachet or not at all, such talk is considered incompatible with a genuine admiration for the classics. Much of Siegel's argument thus rests on the premise that someone who "holds up Stephen King as an example of literary excellence"[210] — which I don't, but never mind — can't possibly be taken seriously. Why didn't I just come out and admit that I hated all great literature? After all, Joyce and DeLillo are both difficult (Siegel's claim, not mine), so how could I like one and not the other? Henry James' plots are slow, so how could I criticize Ha Jin's *Waiting* for being slow? Clearly, I had only praised James "to avoid the appearance of being a philistine."[211] Richard Eder agreed: "These guys always have to have one highbrow writer they like and it's always Henry James."[212]

On the other hand my alleged obsession with action-packed plots, which formed the focus of Eberhart's "A Critic's Manifesto," appears to have been inferred from the first and last few words of my assertion that "modern readers need to see that intellectual content can be reconciled with a vigorous, fast-moving plot." This sentence, as readers will remember, kicks off a brief list of recommendations aimed at showing fans of Harry Potter and the like that real literature, in contrast to the fake stuff, is never boring: *Appointment in Samarra*, *What*

Makes Sammy Run? Hangover Square, *The Second Curtain*, *Gormenghast*, and, from the eighteenth century, *Caleb Williams*. In none of these great novels does "story trump style," none is an easy-to-read "action movie in book form." All of them, on the other hand, deal with "unquantifiable inner experience." But the Defenders of Difficulty would have had to do some reading to know that.

A LESSON IN METHODOLOGY

It is all right to take the first sentence from a Serious Writer's work and to hold it up as evidence of great talent. It is also fine to mock a romance writer on the basis of a few infelicities. It is decidedly *not* all right, however, to advance a dissenting opinion of a Serious Writer's work by discussing the lengthiest, most numerous excerpts that space and copyright law will allow. As Siegel put it, "[Myers'] method of ripping imaginative prose out of its context is foolishly flawed."[213] And here is *The Buffalo News*' Bob Pohl:

> In the case of Annie Proulx...[Myers] pulls a number of short passages out of context and attempts to parse them for sense. Not surprisingly, given the selective nature of the enterprise, they come across as somewhat overwrought...Cormac McCarthy, a novelist with a completely different disposition and temperament, gets a similar treatment in the essay. Myers pulls a couple of well-known passages out of *All the Pretty Horses*, [and] points out how stilted and stylized McCarthy's writing can seem if so excerpted.[214]

But how else could I have discussed these writers' style? Should I have annotated entire pirate editions of *The Shipping News* and *All the Pretty Horses*, and sold them out of the trunk of my car? In any case, I had made clear throughout the Manifesto that the excerpts are worse in context than out of it. It is the unrelenting nature of Proulx's overwroughtness that makes her prose so numbing, just as it is McCarthy's unrelentingly epic tone that makes his novels such ludicrous kitsch. To his credit, Pohl admits that the McCarthy passages I used were well-known, and that even in the rest of the essay I had "sometimes used the same excerpts quoted in favorable reviews."[215] ("Sometimes" was understating things, but I blame myself for not having better emphasized in the first place that the majority of the passages could be found in rave reviews and admiring "scholarship.")

Eder was angrier. "It's ridiculous what he does," he said, "you can find bad writing in any book."[216] Judith Shulevitz chimed in by pronouncing that the "measured" response to my arguments lay in "questioning whether a bad sentence here and there was enough to damn whole novels to oblivion." At the risk of repeating myself, let me point out that "the bad sentence here and there" was often none other than the "evocative" sentence here and there that had once earned the same book a friendly review. The opening passage of *East of the Mountains*, the Toyota Celica scene from *White Noise*, the horse-bowel eulogy from *All the Pretty Horses*, the first sentence from "The Half-Skinned Steer": I wasn't the one who took these things out of context. Nor am I the one who insists on regarding prose in terms of individual sentences instead of as a whole.

In praising my essay in *The Observer*, the British critic Robert McCrum wrote, "Myers is saying nothing that has not been said behind the hand, and out of the corner of the mouth."[217] Indeed, I have little doubt that many of McCrum's American colleagues had always disagreed with the *communis opinio* over at least one or two of the writers featured in my essay; they just hadn't dared to speak their minds in public. When it comes to the twenty or so biggest reputations at any given time a critic must either a) praise novel and novelist b) lament that novel is unworthy of novelist's huge talent, but still a welcome addition to a solid body of work, or c) review someone else's novel instead. We readers know how it works, but editors think we don't know and must never find out. It just wasn't an option for anyone in the U.S., then, to admit the truth of what McCrum had written. But by pretending to believe that there had been a general downgrading of some of my targets well before the Manifesto's appearance, critics could reaffirm their team spirit, present me as ill-informed, and cut loose some of the more vulnerable reputations. At least, that was the plan.

Meghan O'Rourke wrote that for me to complain about Paul Auster, David Guterson and *White Noise* was "a little like pointing out that the emperor's not wearing any clothes after everyone else has noticed."[218] Everyone, eh? The ghastliness of Auster's *Timbuktu* (1999) was glossed over in *The New York Times* and elsewhere with the usual Sentence Cult twaddle about flashes of brilliance; DeLillo's *The Body Artist* (2001) occasioned numerous loving references to *White Noise*; and Guterson's position as one of America's twenty best young novelists (so *Granta* in 1996) was affirmed in the not-as-good-as-his-last-but-look-forward-to-his-next puffery accorded to *East of the Mountains* in 1998. Was that already ancient history?

Of course not. Both Lee Siegel and Judith Shulevitz rushed to defend Auster and DeLillo against my attacks. Which isn't to say that *The New York Times* critic didn't feign some yawns of her own.

> Whatever awards Proulx and Guterson may have won (and the Pulitzer Prize committee is notorious for immortalizing writers of perishable reputation), the two are easily recognizable as the sort of overwrought writers who are eternally popular and frequently forgotten. In reaches of the literary establishment Myers seems unfamiliar with, they have already been discounted as such.[219]

Allow me to point out that Guterson won the PEN/Faulkner Award and no Pulitzer, that Proulx won the PEN/Faulkner and National Book Award *as well as* the Pulitzer, and that neither would have won anything if Shulevitz's own paper hadn't been at the forefront of praising them. But kudos to her and her fellow reviewers for keeping such a tight lid on all that discounting. If anyone before me ever published a critical reappraisal of Guterson's talents it escaped my notice. As for Proulx, her last book before my essay was written prompted *The Washington Post* to declare her the "best prose stylist in the English language"[220] and *The New York Times* to tout her "poetry" and "great writing" in not one but two rave reviews.[221] John Updike even included "The Half-Skinned

Steer" in his anthology of the best American short fiction of the twentieth century.[222] Not bad for a discounted writer.

Perhaps Shulevitz and O'Rourke should have got their stories straight before telling the public who was "in" and who was "out." But they seemed to agree on the most important thing: that we readers must never hold critics accountable for what they write, since it's what they say to each other in exclusive "reaches of the literary establishment" that really counts.

CONSOLING RIDDLES

Charlotte Brontë once wrote, "I believe language to have been given us to make our meaning clear."[223] It's a good thing she's not around today (though I still wish she was), because no part of my essay caused more outrage than this:

> Oprah Winfrey told of calling Toni Morrison to say that she had had to puzzle over many of the latter's sentences. According to Oprah, Morrison's reply was "That, my dear, is called reading." Sorry, my dear Toni, but it's actually called bad writing. Great prose isn't always easy but it's always lucid; no one of Oprah's intelligence ever had to wonder what Joseph Conrad was saying in a particular sentence.

Which prompted Lee Siegel to write:

> Of course you have to puzzle over rare and beautiful sentences! They are the consoling

> riddles that expose the cruel solutions the
> world will throw in your way.[224]

Richard Eder, in a similar vein:

> There are different types of good writing,
> including the kind that's difficult, that you
> bump your head against, and then a few days
> later it dawns on you. And that can change
> your life.[225]

Meghan O'Rourke would say only that my assertion "seems
patently wrong." You'd think these people would have driv-
en home their case with a shining example of Morrison's
prose, but they didn't, nor did they quote anyone else's life-
changing, head-bumping riddles. I wonder why? In fairness,
Siegel did try to put Joyce's famous "ineluctable modality
of the visible" in that category,[226] but in fact it is a perfect
example of the difficult lucidity that is missing from contemporary prose — the kind of writing that rewards the use
of a dictionary instead of punishing it.

Siegel even tried to disprove my remark about
Conrad by offering the following sentence from the great
man's work:

> I felt this was no mere formula of desperate
> speech, but a real alternative in the view of a
> strong soul.

Siegel regards this as "total opacity," which for him is a
good thing, since it helps him to present today's mediocrities as heirs to a glorious tradition of willful obscurity
— and to dismiss me as a rube who is merely feigning

familiarity with the classics.[227] But let's go to the source that Siegel chose not to divulge, namely *The Secret Sharer* (1910), and read that sentence in context:

> The voice was calm and resolute. A good voice.
> The self-possession of that man had somehow
> induced a corresponding state in myself. It was
> very quietly that I remarked:
> "You must be a good swimmer."
> "Yes. I've been in the water practically since
> nine o'clock. The question for me now is
> whether I am to let go this ladder and go on
> swimming till I sink from exhaustion, or — to
> come on board here."
> I felt this was no mere formula of desperate
> speech, but a real alternative in the view of a
> strong soul.[228]

So the strong soul of the young man views swimming until exhaustion as a real alternative to coming on board; he is not simply giving voice to the possibility out of panic. "In the view of" is clumsy, no doubt about it, but it is hardly a puzzling sentence. This leaves me to wonder which of Siegel's claims and implications is the most ludicrous: that the sentence is opaque, that it constitutes great prose *because* it is opaque, that it is representative of Conrad's style, or that it was intended to be puzzling. Surely he knows Conrad's famous words:

> My task which I am trying to achieve is, by
> the power of the written word, to make you
> hear, to make you feel — it is, before all, to
> make you *see*. That — and no more, and it is
> everything.[229]

Indeed it is, and yet Siegel would rather misrepresent Conrad to thousands of readers than allow the likes of me to differ with Toni Morrison. Have the priorities of the American literary critic ever been more neatly demonstrated?

There were also those who misunderstood, or pretended to misunderstand, my opposition to incoherence and obfuscation as an opposition to ambiguity. One man wrote to *The Atlantic Monthly* claiming that I must have a problem with *The Trial* (1925), since we are never told what Joseph K. is accused of.[230] But Kafka clearly knows no more about the charges against Joseph K. than we do; he does not pretend to be keeping the really profound stuff for himself, nor does he try to make us read more into his work than he is capable of thinking. As Nabokov pointed out in criticizing Dostoyevsky's vague references to his characters' past sins, "art is always specific."[231] Literature need not answer every question it raises, but the questions themselves should be clear.

THE HORSES' PERSPECTIVE

Interestingly enough, no attempt was made to argue that the excerpts in "A Reader's Manifesto" deserved the praise originally lavished on them. Instead, critics contented themselves with arguing that at least one or two of the numerous complaints I had made about this or that passage evinced faulty judgment. Did they realize what a feeble point this was? More importantly, did they succeed in making it? You decide. Here is a passage from *White Noise*:

> In the mass and variety of our purchases, in
> the sheer plenitude those crowded bags sug-

gested, the weight and size and number, the familiar package designs and vivid lettering, the giant sizes, the family bargain packs with Day-Glo sales stickers, in the sense of replenishment we felt, the sense of well-being, the security and contentment these products brought to some snug home in our souls — it seemed we had achieved a fullness of being that is not known to people who need less, expect less, who plan their lives around lonely walks in the evening.[232]

About which I had written:

Could the irony be any less subtle? And the tautology: *mass, plenitude, number; well-being, security, contentment*! The clumsy echoes: *size, sizes; familiar, family; sense of, sense of; well-being, being*!...As in the *Toyota Celica* scene, the novel tries to convey the magical appeal of consumerism in prose that is simply flat and tiresome.

Judith Shulevitz defended the excerpt as follows:

Myers misinterprets a passage of DeLillo's celebrating the spiritual comfort of the American supermarket — "the mass and variety of our purchases...the sheer plenitude those crowded bags suggested...the familiar package designs and vivid lettering, the giant sizes, the family bargain packs with Day-Glo stickers." Myers says it is cheap irony. Read in context, though, the passage is the oppo-

110

site. DeLillo's narrator isn't being sarcastic. He's contrasting his shopping basket, over- flowing with jumbo-sized products for his large and happy family, with that of his friend Murray, the lonely bachelor.[233]

And I repeat: could the irony be any less subtle? But per- haps *The New York Times*' "Close Reader" should learn the difference between authorial irony and narratorial sarcasm before weighing in again. Or is she just feigning ignorance? It certainly seems odd that she would edit out the two thirds of the passage where the irony mani- fests itself.

"Some of [Myers'] examples may indeed be pre- tentious," Lee Siegel conceded airily, "but his readings are uncomprehending." The cowboy vomit passage from *All the Pretty Horses* "may have its flaws," he went on — he wouldn't say which — but it was not true that the novel- ist changes point of view in mid-scene:

The whole passage is the narrator's descrip- tion of the horses' 'perspective.'[234]

I confess: I needed a while to realize that this was the start *and* finish of Siegel's argument on this point. Reader had said X, Professional Critic had said Y — ergo Y had been proven. Daniel Atkinson, a biochemistry professor at UCLA, promptly wrote a letter to *The Los Angeles Times* which he was kind enough to send me a copy of:

The horses evidently are versed in Greek mythology, and they (collectively?) sense that "A thing smirking deep in the eyes of grace" lifted itself "like a gorgon in an

111

autumn pool." This is not . . . supple or lean or muscular prose. It is unadulterated nonsense. But Siegel fiercely defends it; it is, he says, "richer language."[235]

Of course, that never made it into print. Siegel and I clashed over another excerpt from the same novel:

He ate the last of the eggs and wiped the plate with the tortilla and ate the tortilla and drank the last of the coffee and wiped his mouth and looked up and thanked her. (McCarthy)[236]

The unpunctuated flow of words bears no relation to the slow, methodical nature of what is being described. (Myers)

Myers is thinking of the act of eating, but in fact, McCarthy is imagining the painful and comic repetition of life's meaningless necessities, which we accomplish in an unthinking blur. (Siegel).

And why repeat tortilla? (Myers)

McCarthy couldn't write "it" because that could refer to the tortilla or the plate. The only alternative would have been . . . describing it in a different way, like this: He ate the last of the eggs and wiped the plate with the tortilla and ate the round thin cake of unleavened cornmeal usually eaten hot with a topping or filling that may include ground meat, cheese and any of various sauces and drank

112

the last of the coffee and wiped his mouth and
looked up and thanked her. (Siegel)[237]

Actually, I had been thinking more along the lines of, "He
ate the last of the eggs and, after a wipe of his plate, the
tortilla," but never mind; Siegel's version is closer to the
spirit of the original.

We also disagreed about Paul Auster's work, and
these excerpts in particular:

> ...and came out as real things, palpable
> objects you could hold in your hand. (Auster,
> *Hand to Mouth*)[238]

> Still and all, Mr. Bones was a dog....he was
> first and foremost the thing he appeared to be.
> Mr. Bow Wow, Monsieur Woof Woof, Sir Cur.
> (Auster, *Timbuktu*)[239]

> Swing the hammer often enough, and you're
> bound to hit the nail on the head — or so the
> logic seems to run. (Myers)

> Tautology is a meaningless or unnecessary
> repetition. But these are not instances of rep-
> etition. They are poetic variations that
> amplify meaning, that draw meaning out into
> another dimension. (Siegel)[240]

I realize there are virtually no two words that mean
exactly the same thing, but how does "could hold in your
hand" draw "palpable" into another dimension? How does
"Monsieur Woof Woof" amplify the meaning of "Mr. Bow
Wow"? It seems cruel to take this seriously.

"In art," Picasso once said, "intentions are not sufficient and, as we say in Spanish: love must be proved by facts and not by reasons. What one does is what counts and not what one had the intention of doing."[241] But America is a kinder place, and as John Mark Eberhart says in English:

> Unlike Myers, I suppose I am more tolerant of writers who at least try to dazzle with language, even if they don't always achieve the kind of grandeur for which they yearn. [242]

Shulevitz reproached me in similarly Pollyannaish terms: "We can roll our eyes at our writers, we can laugh at their moments of baroqueness and vulgarity, but we also get to love them...Hating indiscriminately is a greater sin than loving too much."[243] She also implied that I was oversimplifying things by judging a writer's prose as a whole, instead of searching out the good bits like everyone else. "Are Auster and McCarthy writers of literature or merely 'literary'?" Unsettlingly, they're both...McCarthy can be lucid and heartbreaking in one passage, overblown and windily philosophical in the other."[244] *Salon*'s Laura Miller accused me of "nitpicking," because DeLillo "has written glorious, unforgettable literary riffs, even if his weakness at story and character usually make his books disappointing."[245] I hasten to add that this is mainstream critical opinion; the aesthetic of the half-full glass, or, to be more exact, of the long flat highway relieved by the occasional Stuckey's, can be found even in more scholarly reviews. Here is Pico Iyer recommending *White Noise*:

His atmospherics stronger than his aphorisms, DeLillo occasionally builds up menace without meaning, is about profundity rather than full of it,* becomes — in a word — portentous.... His books mass-produce fortune cookies along with their koans.... Perhaps the oddest and most enduring mystery of DeLillo's remarkable novels is that, though preoccupied with plotting, they are themselves ill-plotted.... Next to DeLillo's large and terrifying talent, most modern fiction seems trifling indeed.[246]

Fiction that is "lucid" and "overblown" in turns, "disappointing" stories interspersed with "glorious riffs," "ill-plotted" novels that "mass-produce fortune cookies along with their koans": this would once have been regarded as damning with faint praise. Now it is the language of advocacy. Just because a book is only intermittently readable, you see, doesn't mean that we shouldn't spend twenty-five dollars on it and read it from cover to cover. We can even make a game out of the bad parts, treating them as "enduring mysteries"; sooner or later another koan will come along to reward us for our patience. Need I add that koans are by definition not profound but nonsensical — and interchangeable? It hardly matters, since it's more about the writers than what they write, and if they fall on their faces half the time, that only makes them more lovable.

But give Iyer credit for the qualifying "modern" in that last sentence. He knows only too well how tiny his boy looks next to, say, Musil, who wouldn't have produced a fortune-cookie if you'd held a gun to his head. It's always safer to compare a mediocrity to his contempo-

* Now, now.

115

raries. As Rick Moody put it recently, with the air of someone making a very daring pronouncement: "After you read *White Noise* you can't go back to reading Tom Robbins and think it's that great."[247]

DECRYING THE BACKWARD GLANCE

I was often criticized, with no textual evidence of course, as laboring under the delusion that in bygone days there were more good books than bad ones. Meghan O'Rourke:

> At any given point in history, there's going to be more bad writing than there is great — or even good — writing. Let's take a look at an earlier time, one that Myers is nostalgic for. In 1900, both *Sister Carrie* and *Lord Jim* were published. Both received critical attention, and neither was a best-seller ... What were the best-selling novels that year? *Unleavened Bread* and *When Knighthood Was in Flower*. Myers' idea of a happier cultural moment, when best-sellers received serious critical attention, is a sentimental lament for an imagined past.[248]

So two good novels were published in 1900, and although both were strong stories told in an unaffected fashion, they still received serious attention from the critics. That sure sounds like a different era to me. The fact that neither of those novels outsold the trash published the same year is irrelevant; Isherwood and Maugham were always outsold too. But if I really did care about best sellers receiving serious attention, or about critically well-received books selling well — and God knows why O'Rourke thinks I do — I would be perfectly happy with the age we live in. *The Shipping News*, *All the Pretty Horses*, and *Snow Falling on Cedars* were all hits with critics and the public alike, as were Charles Frazier's *Cold Mountain* (1997) and Jonathan Franzen's *The Corrections* (2001).

Speaking of Franzen, he offered an *Atlantic Unbound* interviewer a similar interpretation of the Manifesto:

> Myers seems to think that things were different in the past. But I don't think that's true. Look at the Pulitzer Prize winners in the fifties. A certain kind of pretentious, heavy, pseudo-literary writing has been rewarded for a very long time. So my feeling is that there's some truth to his argument, but it was ever thus.[249]

Franzen's implication is that the Pulitzer Prize reflected mainstream critical opinion in the 1950s, which is not true. It was widely disparaged as a middlebrow award, and many prominent critics routinely pounced on its "pseudo-literary" selections as soon as they were announced. These days, however — and this is the Manifesto's point — neither the Sentence Cult nor the division of fiction into "literary" and "genre" camps admits of any distinction between literature and pseudo-literature. Some "literary" works have more good sentences than others, that's all. No wonder, then, that the Pulitzer gang now compiles virtually the same short lists as the National Book Award. (Every so often these juries' selections coincide with a non-"genre" selection from Oprah's Book Club, thereby threatening to revive the middlebrow as a separate category and making things horribly awkward for the "literary" writer involved, most recently Franzen himself.)

Prize committees have always been unreliable judges of quality, not to mention superfluous ones, and any reader silly enough to buy a book for the stamp on the cover deserves a ghastly read, whether it's Mackinlay Kantor's *Andersonville* (Pulitzer Prize, 1956) or Norman Rush's *Mating* (National Book Award, 1991). Still, it's worth noting that there was too much good writing around in the 1950s for even the prize committees to miss. Compare the National Book Award winners from 1950 to 1961 with those from 1990 to 2001, and you will see that things were indeed "different in the past." The names, with one or two exceptions on both sides, speak for themselves.

1950 Nelson Algren	1990 Charles Johnson
1951 William Faulkner	1991 Norman Rush
1952 James Jones	1992 Cormac McCarthy
1953 Ralph Ellison	1993 E. Annie Proulx
1954 Saul Bellow	1994 William Gaddis
1955 William Faulkner	1995 Philip Roth
1956 John O'Hara	1996 Andrea Barrett
1957 Wright Morris	1997 Charles Frazier
1958 John Cheever	1998 Alice McDermott
1959 Bernard Malamud	1999 Ha Jin
1960 Philip Roth	2000 Susan Sontag
1961 Conrad Richter	2001 Jonathan Franzen

Note the last name on the right. As C.S. Lewis wrote, "When our guides unanimously decry / The backward glance, I think we can guess why."[250]

Some of the arguments against the Manifesto never really caught on. Perhaps the strangest was Lee Siegel's claim that:

> Myers has a particular criterion, which grows out of a special gripe.... His main objection to serious fiction is, as he argues in the [National Public Radio] interview, that it does not reflect real life... Myers' argument consists almost entirely of the appeal to "reality." He holds his writers up against this criterion and judges each one a failure.... The most troubling thing about Myers' article is his obdurate clinging to reality as the criterion for judging art. [251]

Needless to say, I have never objected to serious fiction, as opposed to the fake stuff that sees itself in capital letters; Siegel might as well claim that to resist counterfeiting is to object to money. Nor have I ever insisted that literature "reflect real life." I love it when Bulgakov makes a cat talk, and when Gogol dresses a nose in a civil servant's uniform, and — if I may jerk the chain again — when Stephen King gives a car a mind of its own. What I had in fact done during the interview with NPR's *Morning Edition* on July 9, 2001 was point out how absurd it is for the narrator of DeLillo's *The Names*, the usual "elliptical" windbag, to claim that lying about one's destination creates a grave disparity in the listener's brain between the real and the false destination.[252] In making this point I was merely judging *The Names* — as I judge every novel —

by its own standards, in this case as a novel of serious ideas. (DeLillo himself has said that it represents "a deeper level of seriousness."[253]) Not surprisingly, Siegel never explained what *he* thinks the passage means. The fact that I had trusted my own perception of it, instead of respectfully concluding that it was over my head, was all the proof of philistinism he needed.

ROOTLESS COSMOPOLITANISM

How different these attempts at rebuttal would have been had I criticized even one good writer! Let's suppose, for example, that I had taken the unfortunate start to *The Great Gatsby* (1925) — "flabby impressionability" and so on — and used it to argue that F. Scott Fitzgerald was a stilted and pompous fraud. Would Fitzgerald fans have claimed that excerpts may only be used to praise a writer? Would they have dodged the issue by mounting an indignant defense of Great Literature in general? Would they have misrepresented me as a philistine demanding "action movies in book form"? Of course not. The response would have focused squarely on the text itself, which, being a great text, can stand up to anyone's criticism. It would have been child's play to show that the first pages of *The Great Gatsby* are not representative of the novel as a whole, and that Fitzgerald was as far from stilted or pompous as it is possible for a writer to be. But today's reputations are far more delicate things, relying as they do on a combination of reverent skim-reading and literary-historical amnesia. As Charles Jencks once wrote of the camp trend in postmodern architecture: ". . . comparison with the past and a critical temper upset the process at once."[254]

This was what I had set out to do: to upset the process. It was so much more a question of attitude than anything else that an *ad hominem* counterattack was inevitable. While supporters showed little interest in my background, those who disliked the essay logged onto *The Atlantic Monthly*'s website asking for more information about me. Few thought to check the editor's page at the front of the magazine; there was even uncertainty over whether I was a he or a she. Scraps of information were traded back and forth, but they didn't make up enough for anyone to go on. (*The Buffalo News*' Bob Pohl wondered aloud if I was the Brian R. Myers behind two out-of-print poetry books;[255] I am not.) Gerald Howard tried to make something of my home state in his angry letter to *The Atlantic Monthly* — "It may look to Myers from the distance of New Mexico as if," etc. [256] — but all he did was confirm a British newspaper's assertion that part of the backlash had to do with my hailing from a place "way outside the literary loop."[257] Other letters published in the magazine accused me of mean-spiritedness, grumpiness and cruelty.[258] I'm sure some were hoping I would turn out to be a right-wing Republican, like everyone else who uses phrases like "cultural elite," and were disappointed to learn from newspaper reports that I vote Green and wear *Animal Liberation* t-shirts.[259]

But *The New York Times Book Review* wasn't about to give up. At the end of August, Judith Shulevitz called me to ask some seemingly innocent questions about my background. I answered as best I could, believing this to be the preliminary for a real interview, and was just segueing merrily into a discussion of the essay when she said thank you, promised to call back for a quick fact-check — and hung up. She never called back. "Fiction and 'Literary' Fiction," as she called the piece, appeared on

September 9. It begins with a "not another attack on contemporary fiction?"-style yawn, which was no doubt
meant to excuse *The New York Times* for not getting
around to the Manifesto until a month after a dozen
domestic and foreign newspapers had covered it.
Tellingly, though, Shulevitz had to reach back over forty
years for something to compare it to: Dwight Macdonald's
"evisceration" of James Gould Cozzens in 1958.

> Macdonald made use of economics, history
> and sociology to build his case. Myers brings
> only his own sensibility to bear, which is
> emphatically that of the outsider. Myers, who
> lives in New Mexico, is not just a man without
> a stake in the literary establishment. He is
> foreign to it in every way. South African by
> birth and educated as a philologist in
> Germany, the 38-year-old Myers lived until
> recently in China. He told me in a recent
> interview that he plans to spend the coming
> academic year in Seoul, teaching North
> Korean literature to the South Koreans.[260]

Fair enough, I suppose. I'm not South African by birth
but a Fort Dix army brat, and I would probably have
described my job in a way less calculated to evoke the
phrase "selling ice to the eskimos." But I am indeed foreign to the U.S. literary establishment in every way. So?

> If Myers deepened our understanding of the
> American literary condition, it would mean a
> victory for an instinctively appealing kind of
> populism — the globalist kind....He'd have
> proved that a critic needs nothing more than

> taste to make a case. Does Myers' essay do all
> this? It does not, because Myers doesn't have
> a sure grasp of the world he is attacking.... It
> requires either obtuseness or an unfamiliari-
> ty with American culture to ...[261]

Etcetera; it is in this context that Shulevitz makes most of the complaints already discussed. Had I spent less time galli-vanting around the world, and more time at home acquiring a solid grounding in the social sciences, I would have sensed that Proulx and Guterson had already been "discounted," I would have realized Jack Gladney wasn't being "sarcastic" about his shopping cart, and I would have seen the aptness of DeLillo's "send-up of Hitler Studies." These would be minor complaints even if they were valid. Shulevitz also granted me "a knack for identifying bad prose,"[262] which she must realize is a rare gift where she works; if it weren't, Proulx and Guterson would never have been so hyped up in the first place. But with this crowd, it's who you are, not what you write. My essay may have been satisfactory criticism, but to Shulevitz, I wasn't American enough to be a satisfactory critic. At least *The New York Times Book Review* had the decency to run both my own response and a better one from cultural historian Martha Bayles:

> "We can roll our eyes at our writers ... but we
> also get to love them," [Shulevitz] writes. Gee,
> if *we* love 'em, then who is this *foreign* guy to
> knock 'em? This is *American* lit, pal, love it or
> leave it.[263]

But by that time the establishment had already turned its attention to something far more important. No, not the attacks on the World Trade Center, but Jonathan

Franzen's displeasure about having his novel *The Corrections* (2001) selected for Oprah's Book Club. Now *that* was a story.

So much, then, for the response to "A Reader's Manifesto." One question I am often asked is whether I ever heard from the writers I criticized. The answer is no, but it would be unfair to interpret their silence as an admission of defeat or anything else. I wouldn't be surprised, in any case, to find out that they were less bothered by the Manifesto than by the way their supporters went about rebutting it. (DeLillo and Auster, both former expatriates themselves, can only have cringed at *The New York Times*' effort.) To answer another common question: I don't believe that anything I wrote will have much effect on these writers' careers. The public will give them no more thought in twenty years than it gives, say, Norman Rush today, but this will have nothing to do with me, and everything to do with what engendered their reputations in the first place.

In his novel *The Bachelors* (1934), Henry de Montherlant introduces a young woman who, if alive in America today, would have a copy of *The Body Artist* on her bedside table.

> Mlle de Bauret had a taste for literature and the arts, but her literary knowledge only began with the end of the nineteenth century — in other words it was non-existent....[Her] real failing...was that she regarded novelty as synonymous with value. This is a sure sign of barbarism: in any society, it is always the peo-

ple with the lowest intelligence who long to be "in the swim." Incapable of assessing anything by their own taste, culture and discrimination, they automatically judge a problem in accordance with the principle that what is new is true.[264]

The equation of novelty with value is more widespread in America than Europe. It is, in fact, the one thing that our "literary" and "genre" camps have in common: the Clancy fan is no more likely to read Eric Ambler than the Auster fan is likely to read Hermann Broch. But at least the "genre" readers realize that the text is more important than the writer, and they trust solely in their own response to it. Try telling them that someone may not write great thrillers but is still a great thriller writer, or that someone has earned the right to bore them for their own good, or that they should read a half-bad novel because it was ambitiously conceived, and they'll laugh.

Our home-grown Mlles du Bauret are not so secure. They suspend their own "taste, culture and discrimination" because that is what is expected of them, and because there is no other way to get through ten pages of the average prize-winning novel without wanting to fling it across the room. The literary establishment needs more of these people, not fewer, which is why *The New York Times* made such a point of complaining that "Myers brings only his own sensibility to bear," and of declaring I had failed to prove that "a critic needs only taste to make a case."[265] Well, taste and sensibility may not make a professional critic — I have an idea what counts for more in that line of work — but they are all that we readers need to distinguish good books from bad ones. And don't let anyone tell you different.

APPENDIX:

Ten Rules for Serious Writers

TEN RULES FOR "SERIOUS" WRITERS

I. Be Writerly

Read aloud what you have written. If it sounds clear and natural, strike it out. This is the whole of the law; the rest is gloss.

II. Sprawl

Brevity may be the soul of wit, but contemporary reviewers regard a short book as "a slender achievement." So when in doubt, leave it in, even if this means violating rule number one, for as critic James Wood has written, "It is easy, and rightly so, for big books to flush away criticism."[266]

III. Equivocate

The joy of being a writer today is that you can claim your work's flaws are all there by design. Plot doesn't add up? It was never meant to; you were playfully reworking the conventions of traditional narrative. Your philosophizing makes no sense? Well, we live in an incoherent age after all. The dialogue is implausible? Comedy often is. But half the jokes fall flat? Ah! Those were the serious bits. Make sure, then, that your readers can never put a finger on what you are trying to say at any point in the book. Let them create their own text — you're just the one who gets paid for it.

> "We edge nearer death every time we plot. It is
> like a contract that all must sign, the plotters
> as well as those who are the targets of the plot."
>
> Is this true? Why did I say it? What does it
> mean? (DeLillo, *White Noise*)[267]

IV. Mystify

Sometimes mere equivocation isn't enough. Keep readers
in their place by making them think that your mind operates at a higher level. A good example:

> So why is it on Thursday that the men look
> satisfied? Perhaps it's the artificial rhythm of
> the week — perhaps there is something so
> phony about the seven-day cycle the body pays
> no attention to it, preferring triplets, duets,
> quartets, anything but a cycle of seven that
> has to be broken into human parts and the
> break comes on Thursday... [The men in the
> City] seem to achieve some sort of completion
> on that day that makes them steady enough on
> their feet to appear graceful even if they are
> not. (Toni Morrison, *Jazz*)[268]

Granted, men look no more satisfied or graceful on Thurs-
day than on any other day, and even if they did, it would
only prove that the seven-day cycle isn't so phony after all.
But the passage is written with such breezy confidence that
readers blame themselves for not understanding. Just don't
overdo it; it has to look as if *you* know what you mean.

V. Keep Sentences Long

"He got up, went downstairs, and took a taxi." Graham
Greene once used that sentence as an example of how *not*

to write.[269] His fellow-novelist John Braine suggested that a way to improve it would be to have the character leap up from his chair, run downstairs, etcetera.[270] That sort of thing requires a certain skill, however, and if the result is too interesting there is always the danger that critics will take you for a genre hack. A better solution: "He got up and he went downstairs and he took a taxi." Note how the unnatural syntax makes everything sound so much more, well, *literary*. Kent Haruf, author of the acclaimed novel *Plainsong* (1999), shows how it's done. This made it into the excerpt box of *The New York Times*' rave review:

> He went out into the hall again past the closed door and on into the bathroom and shaved and rinsed his face and went back to the bedroom at the front of the house whose high windows overlooked Railroad Street and brought out shirt and pants from the closet and laid them out on the bed and took off his robe and got dressed.[271]

VI. Repeat Yourself

This is a good way to add textual bulk while drawing even more attention to your literary style. There are many variations to choose from. Especially popular is the Faux-Hemingway, which sets the reader's teeth on edge through the eschewal of pronouns (e.g. "wiped his plate with the tortilla and ate the tortilla"), but there's also the Breathless Molly Bloom, or stream-of-consciousness repetition. Like omitting quotation marks, this is a good way to get skim-reading critics to compare you to Joyce.

> I'm worn out begging for chips and putting up
> with librarians who get into a state over turgid
> and I'm looking at the clouds drifting above
> the monument and drifting off myself all
> turgid... (Frank McCourt, *Angela's Ashes*) [272]

Speaking of turgid, there's also the Thesaurus Rex, the stringing together of synonyms. Why waste time agonizing over the perfect word when you can take three words from the same Roget entry and use them all? This received favorable mention in a *New York Times* review:

> But now this hue is vestigial, leftover, a mere
> trace of the era that prevailed here. (Rick
> Moody, *Purple America*.)[273]

"Vestigial," "leftover," "trace": all under "remainder" in your thesaurus. Just because novels should be a chore to read doesn't mean they have to be a chore to write.

VII. Pile On The Imagery

Use metaphors and similes not for vividness — which, like clarity, has a nasty habit of emboldening the reader — but to establish your writerly credentials. A figure of speech left alone is subject to special scrutiny, so make sure to deliver at least two in quick succession. There is no better way to earn praise for your lyrical style.

> We stared out at the city that hummed and
> glittered like a computer chip deep in some
> unknowable machine, holding its secret like a
> poker hand. (Janet Fitch, *White Oleander*)[274]

VIII. *Archaize*

As their letters attest, Civil War soldiers expressed themselves far more clearly and straightforwardly than their
descendants do today. Most Americans, however, prefer to
believe that Melville's idiosyncratic style is an accurate
reflection of nineteenth-century diction, so if your story
is set in this time (or any time before 1970 if it's cowboy
country), use all the archaisms and parallelisms you can.

> The hound and the man fell like-stricken, and
> they moved but little where they fell.
> (Charles Frazier, *Cold Mountain*)[275]

IX Bore

Never underestimate the importance of our puritan tradition; many readers, especially those who had to read *The
Old Man and the Sea* in high school, doubt the value of any
book they don't desperately want to end. The last thing
they will do is complain of boredom, because that might
expose them to imputations of shallowness, poor concentration, or — if the book is meant to be funny — humorless-
ness. So feel free to drone on and on.

> Essentially, what *is* soup? I ask myself. A liq-
> uid food with a meat, fish, or vegetable stock
> as a base and often containing pieces of solid
> food. And then it hits me — why, of course —
> soup is the ideal gastronomic medium for edu-
> cating children about maritime disasters and
> naval battles. For example: Chicken broth
> with little macaroni Titanics and macaroni
> icebergs. Or Hearty Home-Style Battle of
> Trafalgar Bisque with barley Lord Nelsons.
> Defeat of the Spanish Armada Gazpacho.

Cream of Andrea Doria. Battle of Midway Miso
Soup with tofu aircraft carriers and kamikaze
crackers. At the same time I'm exploring the
lyrical possibilities of the 900-number tête-a-
tête.... Now, how to hybridize these two strains
— the pedagogical soups and the erotic phone
conversation — into the germ of a final stanza,
that's the problem. And then it hits me — why,
of course — a sex-talk breakfast cereal with
male and female marshmallow bits each con-
taining an edible, lactose-activated, voice-syn-
thesizing microchip so that...(Mark Leyner,
Tooth Imprints on a Corn Dog)[276]

X. *Play the part*

Take yourself seriously. Practice before the mirror until
you can say things like this with a straight face:

> "It's because I want every little surface to
> shimmer and gyrate that I haven't patience
> for those lax transitional devices of plot, set-
> ting, character, and so on, that characterize a
> lot of traditional fiction." (Mark Leyner)[277]

When asked to write a review, praise your fellow Serious
Writer as you would have him or her praise you. But don't be
afraid to toot your own horn in interviews — like Rick
Moody:

> Some days, you know, I feel this tremendous
> virtuosic talent, like the opening of *Purple
> America*, or the story in *Demonology* called
> "Boys." [278]

Easy does it, though. You want to sell books, but you also want to keep expectations low. Make sure everyone understands that while the English language might have worked for pikers like Shakespeare, it's a couple of sizes too small for what you have to say. Pompous? Sure. But most interviewers are like most readers; the more pompous you act, the more deferential they will become.

> RICK MOODY: My desire to use language to capture emotional and psychic states is always outstripping the ability of this sign system to do its thing. It's always just lying there having only done 80% of the job some-how.

> BILL GOLDSTEIN: And I mean this with respect, but is it the failure of the words or is it the failure of the writer — and I don't mean you in particular, but the ability of any writer? Is it the alchemy between the writer and the words?

> RICK MOODY: Well, I really think that it's built into the system a little bit.... Maybe a tiny bit of sort of semantic disappointment is part of who we are.[279]

ENDNOTES

PREFACE

1. Philip Larkin, Introduction to "All What Jazz," *Required Writing*, 293.
2. Judith Shulevitz, "Fiction and 'Literary' Fiction," *The New York Times*, September 9, 2001.

INTRODUCTION

3. Annie Proulx, *The Shipping News*, 19.
4. Cormac McCarthy, *Blood Meridian*, 44.
5. David Lodge, *The Practice of Writing*, 11.
6. Aldous Huxley, *Those Barren Leaves*, 142-143.
7. James Sutherland (editor), *The Oxford Book of Literary Anecdotes*, 27.
8. Cyril Connolly, *Enemies of Promise*, 85-94.
9. Lee Abbott , "Love in the Back 40," *The New York Times* , November 1, 1987.
10. Herbert Gold , "Reviewmanship and the I-Wrote-A-Book Disease," 571-577.
11. Gold , "Reviewmanship," 573.
12. Gold, "Reviewmanship," 576-577.
13. Gold , "Reviewmanship," 576-577.
14. "Another and Better Ruskin," in *The Essays, Articles and Reviews of Evelyn Waugh*, 466.

EVOCATIVE PROSE

15. Cyril Connolly, *Enemies of Promise*, 89.
16. Annie Proulx, *Close Range: Wyoming Stories*, 9.
17. Fowler, *A Dictionary of Modern English Usage*, "metaphor."
18. John Updike, ed., *The Best American Short Stories of the Century*, 1999.
19. Annie Proulx, "The Half-Skinned Steer, " *In Close Range*, 19.
20. Saul Bellow, *The Adventures of Augie March*, 40.
21. Proulx, *The Shipping News*, 19.
22. Annie Proulx, *Accordion Crimes*, 35.
23. Proulx, *The Shipping News*, 26.
24. Proulx, *The Shipping News*, 193.
25. Proulx, *The Shipping News*, 2.

26. Proulx, *The Shipping News*, 53.
27. Proulx, *The Shipping News*, 9.
28. Proulx, *The Shipping News*, 3.
29. Virginia Woolf, *To The Lighthouse, 155-156.*
30. Proulx, *The Shipping News*, 4.
31. Proulx, *Accordion Crimes*, 370.
32. Walter Kendrick, "The Song of the Squeeze Box," *The New York Times* , June 23, 1996.
33. Richard Eder, "Don't Fence Me In," *The New York Times*, May 23, 1999; John Skow, "On Strange Ground," *Time*, May 17, 1999.
34. Annie Proulx, "The Mud Below," *In Close Range*, 66-67.
35. Eder, "Don't Fence Me In," *The New York Times*, May 23, 1999.
36. Proulx, *Accordion Crimes*, 120.
37. Proulx, *The Shipping News*, 26.
38. Carolyn See, "Proulx's Wild West," *The Washington Post*, July 20, 1999.
39. Eder, "Don't Fence Me In," *The New York Times*, May 23, 1999.
40. Evelyn Waugh, "Fan-fare," 304.
41. Skow, "On Strange Ground," *Time*, May 17 1999.
42. K. Francis Tanabe, *The Washington Post Book Club*, Online Discussion of Annie Proulx , December 27, 1999; See, "Wild West," Dan Cryer, *Newsday,* quoted on the back cover of the paperback version of Annie Proulx's *The Shipping News.*
43. Tanabe, *The Washington Post Book Club*, December 27, 1999.
44. Skow, "On Strange Ground," *Time*, May 17, 1999.
45. Kendrick, "The Song of the Squeeze Box,"*The New York Times*, June 23, 1996.
46. Eder, "Don't Fence Me In," *The New York Times*, May 23, 1999.
47. See, "Wild West," *The Washington Post*, July 20, 1999.
48. Connolly, *Enemies of Promise*, 90.
49. Thomas Wolfe, *Look Homeward, Angel*, 52.

EDGY PROSE

50. Don DeLillo, "Silhouette City: Hitler, Manson and the Millennium," *White Noise : Text and Criticism*, ed. Mark Osteen, 352.
51. Don DeLillo, *White Noise*, 3.
52. Don DeLillo, *White Noise*, 5-6.
53. Caryn James, "I Never Set Out to Write an Apocalyptic Novel," *The New York Times*, April 28, 1985.
54. Don DeLillo, *White Noise*, 155.
55. Cornel Bonca, "Don DeLillo's *White Noise*: The Language of the Species," in *White Noise: Text and Criticism*, Mark Osteen, ed., 469.
56. Paul Maltby, "The Romantic Metaphysics of Don DeLillo ," in *White Noise: Text and Criticism*, ed. Mark Osteen, 501.
57. Christopher Lehmann-Haupt , "Books of the Times," *The New York Times* , January 7, 1985.
58. Don DeLillo, *White Noise*, 20.
59. Anne Brontë, *Agnes Grey*, 1.
60. Don DeLillo, *White Noise*, 63.

61. Don DeLillo, *The Names*, 102-3.

62. Don DeLillo, *White Noise*, 63.

63. Don DeLillo, *The Names*, 189.

64. Don DeLillo, *The Body Artist,* quoted by Maria Russo, "The Body Artist," *Salon,* February 21, 2000.

65. Vince Passaro, "Dangerous Don DeLillo," *The New York Times,* May 19, 1991.

66. Don DeLillo, *White Noise*, 6.

67. Don DeLillo, *Underworld*, 39.

68. DeLillo, *Underworld*, 256.

69. DeLillo, *Underworld*, *260*.

70. DeLillo, *Underworld*, 28.

71. "To become a crowd is to keep out death." DeLillo, *White Noise*, 71.

72. Honore Balzac, *Old Goriot*, trans. Marion Crawford, 7.

73. Honore Balzac, *Lost Illusions*, 166.

74. Honore Balzac, *Old Goriot*, trans. Henry Reed, 104.

75. Balzac, *Old Goriot*, trans. Henry Reed, 114-115.

76. DeLillo, *White Noise* , back jacket flap.

77. DeLillo, *White Noise* , back jacket flap.

78. Jayne Anne Phillips, "Crowding Out Death," *The New York Times,* January 13, 1985.

79. Jay McInerney , quoted on the back cover of Don DeLillo's *Libra.*

80. Phillips, "Crowding Out Death," *The New York Times,* January 13, 1985.

81. DeLillo, *White Noise*, 37-38.

82. Lehmann-Haupt, "Books of the Times," *The New York Times,* January 7, 1985.

83. Rob Swigart, "The Alphabet Obsession," *The San Francisco Chronicle,* October 31, 1982, quoted in introductory pages of Don DeLillo's *The Names,* Vintage Books Editions, 1989.

84. Michiko Kakutani, "Of Death as a Splendid Junk Heap," *The New York Times* , September 16, 1997.

85. Phillips, "Crowding Out Death," *The New York Times,* January 13, 1985.

86. (Author unidentified), *The New Republic* , quoted on the back of *White Noise : Text and Notes.*

87. Lehmann-Haupt, "Books of the Times," *The New York Times,* January 7, 1005.

88. Osteen, ed., "Introduction," in *White Noise : Text and Criticism*, vii-viii.

89. Don DeLillo, *White Noise*, 29.

90. Passaro, "Dangerous Don DeLillo," *The New York Times,* May 19, 1991.

91. Russo, "The Body Artist," *Salon,* February 21, 2000.

92. John Leonard, "The Hunger Artist," *The New York Review of Books,* Feb 22, 2001.

93. Martin Amis, *The War Against Cliché: Essays and Reviews, 1971-2000,* 317.

94. Michael J. Agivino, "DeLillo, Live," *Newsweek,* February 16, 2001.

MUSCULAR PROSE

95. Cormac McCarthy, *The Orchard Keeper*, 7.

96. Cormac McCarthy, *The Crossing* , 354.

97. Ken Follett, *Key to Rebecca*, 17.

98. McCarthy, *Blood Meridian* , 44.

99. McCarthy, *All the Pretty Horses* , 6.

100. McCarthy, *The Crossing*, 6.

101. Robert Hass, "Travels With a She-Wolf," *The New York Times*, June 12, 1994.

102. Cormac McCarthy, *All the Pretty Horses* , 128.

103. McCarthy, *All the Pretty Horses* , 71.

104. McCarthy, *Blood Meridian*, 53-54.

105. McCarthy, *Blood Meridian*, 52.

106. Cormac McCarthy, *Cities of the Plain*, 407.

107. Richard B. Woodward, "Cormac McCarthy's Venomous Fiction,"
     The New York Times, April 19, 1992.

108. McCarthy, *All the Pretty Horses* , 111.

109. McCarthy, *All the Pretty Horses* , 230.

110. McCarthy, *Cities of the Plain*, 253.

111. A.O. Scott, "The Sun Also Sets," *The New York Review of Books*, September 24,
     1998.

112. Sara Mosle, "Don't Let Your Babies Grow Up To Be Cowboys,"
     The New York Times , May 17, 1998.

113. Louis L'Amour, *Hondo*, 12.

114. Louis L'Amour, *Hondo*, 39.

115. L'Amour , appendix to *Hondo*, 180.

116. National Book Award citation, quoted on the back cover of McCarthy's *Cities of the Plain*.

117. Shelby Foote , quoted on back cover of McCarthy's *All the Pretty Horses* .

118. Madison Smartt Bell, "The Man Who Understood Horses," *The New York Times*, May 17, 1992.

119. (Author unidentified), *Village Voice*, quoted on the back cover of McCarthy's *Outer Dark*.

120. Bell, "Man Who Understood," *The New York Times*, May 17, 1992.

121. Hass, "Travels," *The New York Times* , June 12, 1994.

122. Hass, "Travels," *The New York Times* , June 12, 1994.

123. Woodward, "Venomous Fiction," *The New York Times*, April 19, 1992.

SPARE PROSE

124. Paul Auster, *City of Glass*, 194.

125. Auster, *City of Glass*, 133-134.

126. Paul Auster, *Timbuktu* , 55.

127. Paul Auster, *Moon Palace* , 32-33.

128. Auster, *Moon Palace* , 7-8.

129. Auster, *Moon Palace* , 7.

130. Auster, *Timbuktu* , 3.

131. Auster, *Timbuktu*, 35.

132. Auster, *Moon Palace* , 6-7.

133. Auster, *Moon Palace*, 11.

134. Auster, *Moon Palace* , 95-96.

135. Auster, *Timbuktu* , 37.

136. Paul Auster, *Leviathan*, 2.

137. Paul Auster, *Ghosts*, 25.
138. Paul Auster, *Hand to Mouth*, 7.
139. Auster, *Hand to Mouth*, 7.
140. Auster, *Timbuktu*, 35.
141. Michiko Kakutani, "Shamed By Excess, Then Shamed By Too Little," *The New York Times*, September 2, 1997
142. Dennis Drabelle, quoted on the back cover of Auster's *In the Country of Last Things*.
143. (Author unidentified), *Kirkus Review*, quoted on the flap of Auster's *Moon Palace* .
144. (Authors unidentified), *The Sunday Telegraph*, *The Village Voice*, quoted on the flap of Auster's *Moon Palace* .
145. (Authors unidentified), *The Sunday Telegraph*, *Publishers Weekly*, *The Village Voice*, quoted on the flap of Auster's *Moon Palace* ; Michiko Kakutani , "Allusions and Subtext Don't Slow a Good Plot," *The New York Times* , October 2, 1990.
146. Jim Shepard, "This Dog's Life," *The New York Times*, June 20, 1999; Auster, *Timbuktu*, 125.
147. Jim Shepard, "This Dog's Life," *The New York Times*, June 20, 1999; Auster, *Timbuktu*, 125.
148. Michiko Kakutani, "'Dangerous Kiss': Those Lips! Those Eyes! That Mojo's Working!" *The New York Times*, June 13, 1999.
149. A. M. Homes, quoted on dust jacket of Rick Moody's *Purple America*, 1997.
150. Janet Burroway, "Toxic Dreams," *The New York Times*, April 27, 1997.
151. Samuel Beckett, *Malone Dies*, 202-203.
152. Auster, *Moon Palace* , 13.

GENERIC LITERARY PROSE
153. David Guterson, *Snow Falling on Cedars* , 26.
154. David Guterson, *East of the Mountains*, 1.
155. David Guterson, "Aliens," *The Country Ahead of Us, the Country Behind: Stories*, 54.
156. Guterson, *Snow Falling on Cedars* , 345.
157. Guterson, *Snow Falling on Cedars* 98
158. Guterson, "Aliens," *The Country Ahead of Us, the Country Behind: Stories*, 63.
159. Guterson, *East of the Mountains*, 85.
160. James Marcus, review of Guterson's *East of the Mountains*, Amazon.com.
161. Guterson, *Snow Falling on Cedars* , 120.
162. Guterson, *Snow Falling on Cedars* , 69.
163. A.J.A. Symons, *The Quest for Corvo*, 1934, 155.
164. Susan Kenney, "Their Fellow Americans," *The New York Times* , October 16, 1994.
165. Kenney, "Their Fellow Americans," *The New York Times* , October 16, 1994.
166. Donald Keene, *World Within Walls*, 323-327.
167. Shiga Naoya, *A Dark Night's Passing*, 401.
168. Shiga Naoya, "At Kinosaki," *The Paper Door and Other Stories*, 57-64.
169. Linton Weeks, "In the Shadow of 'Cedars'" *The Washington Post* , May 3, 1999.

CONCLUSION

170. Linton Weeks, "Literati, Meet Glitterati: A Shower of Stars at National Book Awards," *The Washington Post* , November 18, 1999.

171. hincklzt@mail2.theonramp.net, "When I was one and twenty . . .", Amazon.com, November 9, 1997.

172. Bill Goldstein, "Let Us Now Praise Books Well Sold, Well Loved, But Seldom Read," *The New York Times*, July 15, 2000.

173. Vince Passaro, "Unlikely Stories: The Quiet Renaissance of American Short Fiction," *Harper's*, October 1999.

174. Rick Moody, *Demonology*, 291.

175. Rick Moody, interview with Bill Goldstein, *The New York Times on the Web*, February 1, 2001.

176. Vince Passaro, "Unlikely Stories," *Harper's*, October 1999.

177. Paul Fussell, *Class*, 144.

178. DeLillo, *Underworld*, 188.

179. Vladimir Nabokov, *Laughter in the Dark*, 16.

180. Vladimir Nabokov, *Bend Sinister*, 60.

181. Philip Larkin, "An Interview With the Observer," *Required Writing,* page 56

182. Saul Bellow, *The Victim,* page 15.

183. Connolly, *Enemies of Promise*, 86.

184. See, "Proulx's Wild West," *The Washington Post*, July 20, 1999.

EPILOGUE: THE RESPONSE TO THE "A READER'S MANIFESTO"

185. *The Wall Street Journal*, "A Reader's Manifesto," July 12, 2001; Ollie Reed Jr., "Readers Vs. Writers: Los Lunas man clobbers 'pretentious' literature in article that stirs international controversy," *The Albuquerque Tribune*, July 26, 2001; Kane Webb, "Feeling unwelcome in the arts? The latest great American critic's name is B.R. Myers, and you've never heard of him. He has a serious complaint about the state of American letters," *The Arkansas Democrat-Gazette*, July 29, 2001; Bill Eichenberger, "Knee-jerk Reviews of Modern Fiction Miss What It Means,"*The Columbus Dispatch*, July 29, 2001; Robert McCrum, "The End of Literary Fiction," *The Observer*, August 5, 2001; Amanda Craig, "Have Our Literary Darlings Lost The Plot?" *The Sunday Times*, July 15, 2001; Joanna Coles, "Stephen King Dismissed as Mere 'Storyteller,'" *The Times of London*, July 9, 2001.

186. Jonathan Yardley, "The Naked and the Bad," *The Washington Post*, July 2, 2001.

187. B.R. Myers, "A Reader's Manifesto," *The Australian Financial Review*, August 17 (part 1) and August 24, 2001 (part 2).

188. Peter Holbrook, "If It Sucks, Say It," *The Australian*. October 3, 2001.

189. Mursi Saad El-Din, "Plain Talk," *Al-Ahram Weekly*. July 19-25, 2001.

190. Mary McNamara, "For Prose Warrior, Lit'rature is the Enemy," *The Los Angeles Times*, July 16, 2001.

191. Michael Dirda, "Dirda on Books," *WashingtonPost.com Live Online*, June 28, 2001.

192. Dirda, "Dirda on Books," *WashingtonPost.com Live Online,* July 5, 2001.

193. Dirda, "Dirda on Books," *WashingtonPost.com Live Online,* July 12, 2001.

194. McNamara, "Prose Warrior," *The Los Angeles Times*. July 16, 2001.

195. Tom Wolfe, "Stalking the Billion-Footed Beast: A literary manifesto for the new social novel," *Harper's Magazine*, November 1989.

196. Unsigned, "LAT Botches Attack on 'A Reader's Manifesto,'" L.A. Examiner, July 29, 2001.

197. Meghan O'Rourke, "Unfair Sentence: The Case for Difficult Books," *Slate*, July 27, 2001; John Mark Eberhart, "A Critic's Manifesto," *The Kansas City Star*, July 29 and August 5, 2001; Bob Pohl, "'Writerly Prose' Takes Some Lumps," *The Buffalo News*, August 5, 2001; Laura Miller, "Sentenced to Death," *Salon*, August 16, 2001.

198. Judith Shulevitz, "Fiction and 'Literary' Fiction," *The New York Times Book Review*, September 9, 2001.

199. T. Coraghessan Boyle, Message Board, www.tcboyle.com, July 12, 2001.

200. McNamara, "Prose Warrior," *The Los Angeles Times*, July 16, 2001.

201. O'Rourke, "Unfair Sentence," *Slate*, July 27.

202. Eberhart, "A Critic's Manifesto," *The Kansas City Star*, July 29 and August 5, 2001.

203. Dirda, "Dirda on Books," *WashingtonPost.com Live Online*, June 28, 2001.

204. Lee Siegel, "Why Great Literature Contains Everything But a Clear Answer," *The Los Angeles Times*, July 29, 2001.

205. Dan Cryer, "Letters," *The Atlantic Monthly*, November 2001.

206. O'Rourke, "Unfair Sentence," *Slate*, July 27.

207. Siegel, "Great Literature," *The Los Angeles Times*, July 29, 2001.

208. Gerald Howard, "Letters," *The Atlantic Monthly*, November 2001.

209. Miller, "Sentenced to Death," *Salon*, August 16, 2001.

210. Siegel, "Great Literature," *The Los Angeles Times*, July 29, 2001.

211. Siegel, "Great Literature," *The Los Angeles Times*, July 29, 2001.

212. McNamara, "Prose Warrior," *The Los Angeles Times*, July 16, 2001.

213. Siegel, "Great Literature," *The Los Angeles Times*, July 29, 2001.

214. Pohl, "'Writerly Prose,'" *The Buffalo News*, August 5, 2001.

215. Pohl, "'Writerly Prose,'" *The Buffalo News*, August 5, 2001.

216. McNamara, "Prose Warrior," *The Los Angeles Times*, July 16, 2001.

217. McCrum, "The End of Literary Fiction," *The Observer*, August 5, 2001.

218. O'Rourke, "Unfair Sentence," *Slate*, July 27.

219. Shulevitz, "Fiction and 'Literary' Fiction," *The New York Times*, September 9, 2001.

220. See, "Wild West," *The Washington Post*, July 20, 1999.

221. Eder, "Don't Fence Me In," *The New York Times*, May 23, 1999; Christopher Lehmann-Haupt, "Lechery and Loneliness in the American West," *The New York Times*, May 12, 1999.

222. Updike, ed., *The Best American Short Stories of the Century*, 1999.

223. Charlotte Brontë (writing as Currer Bell), "Biographical Notice of Ellis and Acton Bell," xl.

224. Siegel, "Great Literature," *The Los Angeles Times*, July 29, 2001.

225. McNamara, "Prose Warrior," *The Los Angeles Times*, July 16, 2001.

226. Siegel, "Great Literature," *The Los Angeles Times*, July 29, 2001.

227. Siegel, "Great Literature," *The Los Angeles Times*, July 29, 2001.

228. Joseph Conrad, *The Secret Sharer*, 9.

229. Joseph Conrad, preface to *The Nigger of the Narcissus*, 14.

230. Marl Doussard, "Letters," in *The Atlantic Monthly*, October 2001.

231. Vladimir Nabokov, *Lectures on Russian Literature*, 117.

232. DeLillo, *White Noise*, 20.

233. Shulevitz, "Fiction and 'Literary' Fiction," *The New York Times*, September 9, 2001.

234. Siegel, "Great Literature," *The Los Angeles Times*, July 29, 2001.

235. Daniel Atkinson, "Letter to the Editor," *Los Angeles Times*, August 18, 2001

236. McCarthy, *The Crossing*, 354.

237. Siegel, "Great Literature," *The Los Angeles Times*, July 29, 2001.

238. Auster, *Hand to Mouth*, 7.

239. Auster, *Timbuktu*, 35.

240. Siegel, "Great Literature," *The Los Angeles Times*, July 29, 2001.

241. Marius de Zayas, "Picasso Speaks," *The Arts*, 1923.

242. Eberhart, "A Critic's Manifesto," *The Kansas City Star*, July 29 and August 5, 2001.

243. Shulevitz, "Fiction and 'Literary' Fiction," *The New York Times*, September 9, 2001.

244. Shulevitz, "Fiction and 'Literary' Fiction," *The New York Times*, September 9, 2001.

245. Miller, "Sentenced to Death," *Salon*, August 16, 2001.

246. Pico Iyer, "A Connoisseur of Fear," *Partisan Review*, 53 (1986), 382-3.

247. Rick Moody, quoted in "The Novelist of the Now," *Esquire*, February 2001, 115.

248. O'Rourke, "Unfair Sentence," *Slate*, July 27.

249. Jonathan Franzen, interviewed by Jessica Murphy, "Mainstream and Meaningful," *Atlantic Unbound*, October 3, 2001.

250. C. S. Lewis, "On a Vulgar Error," in *Poems*, 60.

251. Siegel, "Great Literature," *The Los Angeles Times*, July 29, 2001.

252. B.R. Myers, interviewed by Renee Montagne, "Morning Edition," *National Public Radio*, July 9, 2000.

253. Bonca "Don DeLillo's White Noise: The Language of the Species," in *White Noise: Text and Criticism*, Mark Osteen, ed., 475.

254. Charles Jencks, *Modern Movements in Architecture*, 204.

255. Pohl, "'Writerly Prose,'" *The Buffalo News*, August 5, 2001.

256. Howard, "Letters," *The Atlantic Monthly*, October 2001

257. Joanna Coles, "Stephen King, though both intellectual and popular, is dismissed by the American literati as a mere 'storyteller,'" *The Times of London*, July 9, 2001.

258. " Letters," *The Atlantic Monthly*, November 2001.

259. Kane Webb, "Feeling unwelcome in the arts?", *Arkansas Democrat-Gazette*, July 29, 2001; Ollie Reed Jr., *The Albuquerque Tribune*, "Readers Vs. Writers," July 26 2001.

260. Shulevitz, "Fiction and 'Literary' Fiction," *The New York Times*, September 9, 2001.

261. Shulevitz, "Fiction and 'Literary' Fiction," *The New York Times*, September 9, 2001.

262. Shulevitz, "Fiction and 'Literary' Fiction," *The New York Times*, September 9, 2001.

263. Martha Bayles, "Letters," *The New York Time Book Reviews*, September 30, 2001.

264. Henry de Montherlant, *The Bachelors*, 90-91.

265. Shulevitz, "Fiction and 'Literary' Fiction," *The New York Times*, September 9, 2001

APPENDIX:

TEN RULES FOR SERIOUS WRITERS

266. James Wood, "Black Noise," *The New Republic*, November 10, 1997.

267. DeLillo, *White Noise,* 26.

268. Toni Morrison, *Jazz*, 50.

269. Graham Greene, quoted in John Braine , *Writing a Novel*, 50.

270. John Braine , *Writing a Novel*, 50.

271. Kent Haruf, *Plainsong* , 4. (Quoted in "Eyes Covered But Seeing, A Novelist Looks Inward," Dinitia Smith, *The New York Times* , December 1, 1999.)

272. Frank McCourt , *Angela's Ashes*, 305.

273. Moody, *Purple America*, 25.

274. Janet Fitch, *White Oleander*, 3.

275. Charles Frazier, *Cold Mountain, 349.*

276. Mark Leyner, *Tooth Imprints on a Corn Dog*, 158-159.

277. Mark Leyner, quoted in *Postmodern American Fiction: A Norton Anthology*, page 241-242.

278. Rick Moody, interviewed by Bill Goldstein, *The New York Times on the Web*, February 1, 2001.

279. Rick Moody, interviewed by Bill Goldstein, *The New York Times on the Web*, February 1, 2001.

BIBLIOGRAPHY

Abbott, Lee. "Love in the Back 40." *The New York Times*, November 1, 1987.

Agivino, Michael J. "DeLillo, Live." *Newsweek*. February 16, 2001.

Amis, Martin. "*Underworld* by Don DeLillo." In *The War Against Cliché: Essays and Reviews, 1971-2000*. Hyperion, New York, 2001. 316-321.

Auster, Paul. *Ghosts: The New York Trilogy, Vol. 2*. Sun & Moon Press, Los Angeles, 1986.

Auster, Paul. *Hand to Mouth: A Chronicle of Early Failure*. Henry Holt & Co., New York, 1997.

Auster, Paul. *In the Country of Last Things*. Viking Penguin, New York, 1987.

Auster, Paul. *Leviathan*. Viking Penguin, New York, 1992.

Auster, Paul. *Moon Palace*. Viking Penguin, New York, 1989.

Auster, Paul. *The Music of Chance*. Viking Penguin, New York, 1992.

Auster, Paul. *Timbuktu*. Henry Holt & Co., New York, 1999.

"Bad Books, Good Reviews." *Morning Edition*, National Public Radio. July 6, 2001.

Balzac, Honoré de. *Old Goriot*, trans. Marion Crawford, Penguin Books, London, 1951.

Balzac, Honoré de. *Old Goriot*, trans. Henry Reed, Signet Classics, New York, 1962

Balzac, Honoré de. *Lost Illusions*, trans. Herbert Hunt, Penguin Books, London, 1971.

Beckett, Samuel. *The Beckett Trilogy*. Picador, New York, 1980.

Bell, Madison Smartt. "The Man Who Understood Horses." *New York Times*, May 17, 1992.

Bellow, Saul. *The Adventures of Augie March*. Penguin Books, New York, 1984.

Bellow, Saul. *The Victim*. Vanguard, New York, 1947.

The Best American Short Stories of the Century. Edited by John Updike, co-edited by Katrina Kenison. Houghton Mifflin Co., Boston, 1999.

Birkerts, Sven. "Carver's Last Stand." *Atlantic Unbound*, January 24, 2001.

Bonca, Cornel. "Don DeLillo's *White Noise*: The Language of the Species." In *White Noise: Text and Criticism*, edited by Mark Osteen. Viking Books, New York, 1998. 456-479.

Boyle, T.C. "Re: Interesting *Atlantic Monthly* Article." On T. Coraghessan Boyle Message Board, www.tcboyle.com. July 12, 2001.

Braine, John. *Writing a Novel*. McGraw-Hill, New York, 1975.

Brontë, Anne. *Agnes Grey*. Oxford University Press, Oxford, 1998.

Brontë, Charlotte. (Currer Bell) "Biographical Notice of Ellis and Acton Bell." In *Wuthering Heights*. Penguin USA, New York, 1996. xxxvi – xlii.

Burroway, Janet. "Toxic Dreams." *The New York Times*. April 27, 1997.

Coles, Joanna. "Stephen King Dismissed as Mere 'Storyteller.'" *The Times of London*. July 9, 2001.

Connolly, Cyril. *Enemies of Promise*. André Deutsch, London, 1996.

Conrad, Joseph. *The Nigger of the Narcissus*. Doubleday & Co., New York, 1914.

Conrad, Joseph. *The Secret Sharer*. Penn State Electronic Classics Series Publication, 2000.

Craig, Amanda. "Have Our Literary Darlings Lost The Plot?" *The Sunday Times* (UK). July 15, 2001.

Crawford, Marion. "Introduction" to her translation of *Old Goriot*, Honoré de Balzac, Penguin Books, London, 1951. 5-24.

DeLillo, Don. *Libra*. Viking Penguin. New York, 1988.

DeLillo, Don. *Mao II*. Viking Penguin, New York, 1991.

DeLillo, Don. *The Names*. Vintage Books. New York, 1989.

DeLillo, Don. "Silhouette City: Hitler, Manson and the Millennium." In *White Noise: Text and Criticism*, edited by Mark Osteen. Viking Books, New York, 1998. 344-352.

DeLillo, Don. *Underworld*. Scribner, New York, 1997.

DeLillo, Don. *White Noise*. Viking Penguin, New York, 1985.

Dirda, Michael. "Dirda on Books." *Washington Post Online*. June 28, 2001; July 5, 2001; July 12, 2001.

Eberhart, John Mark. "A Critic's Manifesto." *The Kansas City Star*. July 29, 2001 (Part I) and August 5, 2001 (Part II).

Eder, Richard. "Don't Fence Me In." New York Times, May 23, 1999.

Fitch, Janet. *White Oleander*. Little, Brown & Co., New York, 1999.

Eichenberger, Bill. "Knee-jerk Reviews of Modern Fiction Miss What It Means." *The Columbus Dispatch*. July 29, 2001.

El-Din, Mursi Saad. "Plain Talk." *Al-Ahram Weekly*. July 19-25, 2001.

Follett, Ken. *The Key to Rebecca*. William Morrow, New York, 1980.

Fowler, H.W. *A Dictionary of Modern English Usage*. Oxford University Press, Oxford, 1965.

Frazier, Charles. *Cold Mountain*. Atlantic Monthly Press, New York, 1997.

Fussell, Paul. *Class: A Guide Through the American Status System*. Summit Books, New York, 1983.

Gold, Herbert. "Reviewmanship and the I-Wrote-A-Book Disease," in *Highlights from 125 Years of the Atlantic*, The Atlantic Monthly Company [Atlantic Subscriber Edition], 1977. 571-577.

Goldstein, Bill, "Audio Interview: Rick Moody," *The New York Times on the Web*, February 1, 2001.

Goldstein, Bill, "Let Us Now Praise Books Well Sold, Well Loved, But Seldom Read." *The New York Times*, July 15, 2000.

Guterson, David. "Aliens," in *The Country Ahead of Us, the Country Behind: Stories*. Vintage Books, New York, 1989. 45-63.

Guterson, David. *East of the Mountains*. Harcourt Brace and Company, 1998.

Guterson, David. *Snow Falling on Cedars*. Harcourt Brace and Company, New York, 1994.

Haruf, Kent. *Plainsong*. Knopf, New York, 1999.

Hass, Robert. "Travels With a She-Wolf." *The New York Times*, June 12, 1994.

Hemingway, Ernest. *Death in the Afternoon*. Charles Scribner's Sons, New York, 1960.

Hemingway, Ernest. "In Another Country," in *The Short Stories of Ernest Hemingway*. Charles Scribner's Sons, New York, 1938. 267-272.

Holbrook, Peter. "If It Sucks, Say It." *The Australian*. October 3, 2001.

Howard, Gerald. "The American Strangeness: An Interview with Don DeLillo." *Hungry Mind Review*, 1997.

Huxley, Aldous. *Those Barren Leaves*. Dalkey Archive Press, Normal, IL., 1998 (first published 1925).

Iyer, Pico. "A Connoisseur of Fear." *Partisan Review*, 53 (1986). 379-384.

James, Caryn. "I Never Set Out to Write an Apocalyptic Novel." *The New York Times*, April 28, 1985.

James, Caryn. "Is Everybody Dead Around Here?" *The New York Times*, April 28, 1985.

Jencks, Charles. *Modern Movements In Architecture*. Doubleday, New York, 1973.

Kakutani, Michiko. "Allusions and Subtext Don't Slow a Good Plot." *The New York Times*, October 2, 1990.

Kakutani, Michiko. "Of America as a Splendid Junk Heap." *The New York Times*, September 16, 1997.

Kakutani, Michiko. "Shamed By Excess, Then Shamed By Too Little." The New York Times, September 2, 1997.

Kakutani, Michiko. "'Dangerous Kiss': Those Lips! Those Eyes! That Mojo's Working!" *The New York Times*, June 13, 1999.

Keene, Donald. *World Within Walls: Japanese Literature of the Pre-Modern Era 1600-1867*. Charles E. Tuttle Company, Tokyo, 1978.

Kendrick, Walter. "The Song of the Squeeze Box." *The New York Times*, June 23, 1996.

Kenney, Susan. "Their Fellow Americans." *The New York Times*, October 16, 1994.

L.A. Examiner. "LAT Botches Attack on 'A Reader's Manifesto.'" July 29, 2001.

L'Amour, Louis. *Hondo*. Bantam Books, New York, 1997.

Larkin, Philip. *Required Writing: Miscellaneous Pieces 1955-1982*. Farrar Straus Giroux. New York, 1982.

Lehmann-Haupt, Christopher. "Books of the Times: *White Noise*." *The New York Times*, January 7, 1985.

Lehmann-Haupt, Christopher. "Lechery and Loneliness in the American West." *The New York Times*, May 12, 1999.

Leonard, John. "The Hunger Artist." *The New York Review of Books*. February 22, 2001.

Leyner, Mark. *Tooth Imprints on a Corn Dog*. Random House, New York, 1995.

Lewis, C.S. "On a Vulgar Error." In *Poems*, edited by Walter Hooper. Harvest Books. New York, 1997. 60.

Lodge, David. *The Art of Fiction*. Penguin, London, 1992.

Lodge, David. The Practice of Writing. Allen Lane, New York, 1997.

Maltby, Paul. "The Romantic Metaphysics of Don DeLillo." In *White Noise: Text and Criticism*. 498-514.

McCarthy, Cormac. *All the Pretty Horses*. Knopf, New York, 1993.

McCarthy, Cormac. *Blood Meridian, or the Evening Redness in the West*. Random House, New York, 1985.

McCarthy, Cormac. *Cities of the Plain*. Knopf, New York, 1998.

McCarthy, Cormac. *The Crossing*. Vintage International, New York, 1995.

McCarthy, Cormac. *The Orchardkeeper*. Vintage International, New York, 1993.

McCarthy, Cormac. *Outer Dark*. Vintage International, New York, 1993.

McCarthy, Cormac. *Suttree*. Vintage International, New York 1992.

McCourt, Frank. *Angela's Ashes*. Scribner, New York, 1996.

McCrum, Robert. "The end of literary fiction." *The Observer*. August 5, 2001.

McNamara, Mary. "For Prose Warrior, Lit'rature is the Enemy." *The Los Angeles Times*. July 16, 2001.

Miller, Laura. "Sentenced to Death." *Salon*, August 16, 2001.

Mitgang, Herbert. "Boys on Horseback, Loose in Mexico." *The New York Times*, May 27, 1992.

Montherlant, Henry de. *The Bachelors*. Translated from the French by Terence Kilmartin. MacMillan, New York, 1960.

Moody, Rick. *Demonology*. Little, Brown and Company, New York, 2001.

Moody, Rick. *Purple America*. Little, Brown and Company, New York, 1994.

Morrison, Toni. *Jazz*. Knopf, New York, 1992.

Mosle, Sara. "Don't Let Your Babies Grow Up To Be Cowboys." *The New York Times*, May 17, 1998.

Murphy, Jessica. "Mainstream and Meaningful." (Interview with Jonathan Franzen) *Atlantic Unbound*. October 3 2001.

Nabokov, Vladimir. *Bend Sinister*. Vintage International, New York, 1990.

Nabokov, Vladimir. *Laughter in the Dark*. Vintage International, New York, 1989.

Nabokov, Vladimir. *Lectures on Russian Literature*. Edited by Fredson Bowers. Harcourt Brace Jovanovich, New York, 1981.

O'Rourke, Meghan. Unfair Sentence: "The Case for Difficult Books." *Slate*. July 27, 2001.

The Oxford Book of Literary Anecdotes. Edited by James Sutherland. Clarendon Press, Oxford, 1975.

Passaro, Vince. "Dangerous Don DeLillo." *The New York Times Magazine*. May 19, 1991.

Passaro, Vince. "Unlikely Stories: The Quiet Renaissance of American Short Fiction." *Harper's*, October 1999.

Phillips, Jayne Anne. "Crowding Out Death." *The New York Times*, January 13, 1985.

Pohl, Bob. "'Writerly Prose' Takes a Few Lumps." *The Buffalo News*, August 5, 2001.

Postmodern American Fiction: A Norton Anthology. Edited by Paula Geyh, Fred G. Leebron and Andrew Levy. Norton, New York, 1997.

Proulx, Annie. *Accordion Crimes*. Scribner, New York 1996.

Proulx, Annie. *Close Range: Wyoming Stories*. Scribner, New York, 1999. "The Half-Skinned Steer," 19-38. "The Mud Below," 41-78.

Proulx, Annie. *The Shipping News*. Scribner, New York, 1993.

Proust, Marcel. Remembrance of Things Past. Translated by C. K. Scott Montcrieff and Terence Kilmartin. Vintage Books, New York, 1982.

Reed, Jr., Ollie. "Los Lunas Man Clobbers 'Pretentious' Literature in Article that Stirs International Controversy," *Albuquerque Tribune*, July 26, 2001.

Robinson, Roxana. "The End of the Road." *The Washington Post*, May 2, 1999.

Russo, Maria. "'The Body Artist' by Don DeLillo." *Salon*. February 21, 2001.

Scott, A.O. "The Sun Also Sets." *The New York Review of Books*. September 24, 1998.

See, Carolyn. "Proulx's Wild West. Talent as Big As the Wyoming Sky." *The Washington Post*, July 20, 1999.

Shulevitz, Judith. "Fiction and 'Literary' Fiction." *The New York Times Book Review*. September 9, 2001.

Shepard, Jim. "This Dog's Life." *The New York Times*, June 20, 1999.

Shiga Naoya. *A Dark Night's Passing*, translated by Edwin McLellan, Kodansha, Tokyo, 1986.

Shiga Naoya. "At Kinosaki," in *The Paper Door and Other Stories*, translated by Lane Dunlop. Tuttle, Tokyo, 1992.

Siegel, Lee. "Why Great Literature Contains Everything But a Clear Answer." *The Los Angeles Times Book Review*. July 29, 2001.

Skow, John. "On Strange Ground." *Time*. May 17, 1999.

Smith, Dinitia. "Eyes Covered But Seeing, A Novelist Looks Inward." *The New York Times*, December 1, 1999.

Symons, A.J.A. *The Quest for Corvo: An Experiment in Biography*. The MacMillan Company. New York, 1934.

Tanabe, K. Francis. Opening remarks to "The Washington Post Book Club, Online Discussion on Annie Proulx," December 27, 1999.

Wall Street Journal. "A Reader's Manifesto (editorial)." July 12, 2001.

Waugh, Evelyn. *The Essays, Articles and Reviews of Evelyn Waugh*, edited by Donat Gallagher. Little, Brown and Company, London, 1983.

Webb, Kane. "Feeling unwelcome in the arts? The latest great American critic's name is B.R. Myers, and you've never heard of him. He has a serious complaint about the state of American letters." *The Arkansas Democrat-Gazette*. July 29, 2001.

Weeks, Linton. "In the Shadow of Cedars: Guterson's First Novel Casts a Pall on the Second." *The Washington Post*. May 3, 1999.

Weeks, Linton. "Literati Meet Glitterati: A Shower of Stars at National Book Awards." *The Washington Post*, November 18, 1999.

Wolfe, Thomas. *Look Homeward, Angel*. Collier Books, New York, 1957.

Wolfe, Tom. "Stalking the Billion-Footed Beast." *Harper's*, November 1989.

Wood, James. "Black Noise." *The New Republic*. November 10, 1997.

Woodward, Richard B. "Cormac McCarthy's Venomous Fiction." *The New York Times*. April 19, 1992.

Woolf, Virginia. *To The Lighthouse*. Harcourt, Brace and World, New York, 1955.

Yardley, Jonathan. "The Naked and the Bad." *The Washington Post*. July 2, 2001.

Zayas, Marius de. "Picasso Speaks." (Interview) *The Arts* 3 (no. 5), New York, 1923.

B.R. Myers was born in the US but raised in Bermuda, South Africa and Germany. He teaches North Korean studies in South Korea.